The Way of The Cross

Suffering Selfhoods in the Roman Catholic Philippines

JULIUS BAUTISTA

 University of Hawai'i Press

Honolulu

Printed in the United States of America

Library of Congress Cataloging-in-Publication Data

Names: Bautista, Julius, author.
Title: The way of the cross : suffering selfhoods in the Roman Catholic
    Philippines / Julius Bautista.
Description: Honolulu : University of Hawai'i Press, 2019. | Includes
    bibliographical references and index.
Identifiers: LCCN 2019021390 | ISBN 9780824879976 (cloth)
Subjects: LCSH: Catholic Church—Philippines—Pampanga—Customs and
    practices. | Scourging of Christ, Devotion to—Philippines—Pampanga. |
    Flagellation—Philippines—Pampanga. | Pampanga (Philippines)—Religious
    life and customs.
Classification: LCC BX2159.S37 B38 2019 | DDC 306.6/6392509599—dc23
LC record available at https://lccn.loc.gov/2019021390

ISBN 978-0-8248-9247-0 (paperback)

Cover art: (Front) Filipino Roman Catholics submit themselves to be nailed to
crosses on Good Friday, San Pedro, Cutud. Photo by author. (Spine and back)
The Via Crucis (Way of the Cross) is a yearly theatrical ritual in which an actor
playing the title role of "Kristo" is nailed to the cross in commemoration of
Jesus Christ's Passion and involvement in ordinary people's lives. Photo by
Leonardo Calma.

Cover design: Michael Y. Cueva

University of Hawai'i Press books are printed on acid-free paper and meet the
guidelines for permanence and durability of the Council on Library Resources.

Introduction

An Ethnography of Suffering Selfhood

This book is about the Roman Catholic religious rituals that take place in the Philippine province of Pampanga during the Christian Holy Week. During this time, hundreds of men and women undergo acts of self-inflicted pain in ways that commemorate the "Way of the Cross": the torment and crucifixion that Christ endured in the last days of his earthly existence. Collectively, these acts are called Passion rituals, and in this book the ethnographic focus is on three in particular: the *pabasa* (a "reading"), in which groups of people endure long hours of continuously chanting Christ's Passion story; the *pagdarame* ("to empathize"), in which hundreds of people self-flagellate onto open wounds on their backs as they go on a walking journey around the province; and the *pamamaku king krus* ("nailing on the cross"), in which steel nails are driven through the palms and feet of ritual practitioners. A commonly made assumption about these rituals is that excruciating pain is inflicted in order to perfectly imitate Christ and to achieve atonement for one's sins, which are conditions that would ostensibly bring one closer to the ultimate reward of spiritual transcendence in the afterlife. However, I have found that many Passion ritual practitioners think about their actions differently. What those who perform these rituals consistently evoke is a desire to cultivate a kind of intimacy with God that places them and their loved ones in the best position to receive His divine favor in this life, here and now.

A sense of my ethnographic encounter would serve to convey why such immanently framed ritual motivations are both interesting and perplexing. In the course of doing fieldwork in Pampanga, I met a man named Jackson who, every year on Good Friday, has himself nailed to a cross. Jackson is among the most recognizable ritual nailees, or *namamaku*, in Pampanga. In Holy Week 2012, I stood but a few feet from him as four-inch steel nails were driven through his hands, deep enough to fasten them to the wooden cross beneath. Jackson let out a wail at the moment the nails punctured the meaty part of his flesh, causing him to convulse involuntarily from what he would later describe as a "sharp, intense pain [that shoots] all the way from the hand to the elbow." Yet as Jackson hung on the cross for a good fifteen minutes, one could observe a calmness and serenity to his countenance, even while the muscles in his hands and upper arms remained tense and twitching. Like most of the namamaku

I spoke with in Pampanga, Jackson never denies that the experience of nailing is extremely painful. It is how he characterizes pain that tends to surprise those who ask about his religious commitments: nailing on the cross, he says, is not about imitating Christ or atoning for his own sinfulness so that he would go to heaven. It is, rather, about suffering for the prosperity and good health of his family. In this sense, the pain that he feels from being nailed to the cross is *"maginhawa,"* which he explains as a feeling of great relief and almost ecstatic sense of release.

To those who witness nailing rituals, whether in the flesh or on TV, the initial response may be one of bewilderment at the incongruity between such a terribly painful experience and an expression of contentment. Intuitively, it is hard to believe that self-inflicted physical pain might have any positive valence at all, regardless of its religious motivations. This is because we are conditioned by what sociologists of religion Chris Shilling and Philip Mellor described as the "medical colonisation" of polypharmacy, in which pain is posited as a negative experience that can and should be "muted" upon the administration of a host of anesthetic and medicinal regimens (Shilling and Mellor 2010, 523). As the philosopher of religion Sarah Coakley (2009) has suggested, with the progress of medicine, "we've come to see not just pain but suffering and death and all of those things, as things that we can potentially get rid of, and I think that it makes our culture the poorer for it, because you know, when we try and obliterate suffering, we can end up obliterating pleasure as well." Granting the pervasiveness of this biomedical paradigm, it would be understandable that many of us would be taken aback by the notion that anyone should experience pain at all, let alone inflict it upon oneself, when pain is something that is regularly and effectively treated, managed, and alleviated.

Our bafflement of Jackson's positive pain experience is intensified by the fact that Roman Catholic religious authorities deem it completely unnecessary for the "proper" fulfillment of religious obligations. Most Passion rituals that are performed in Pampanga are officially disavowed by the Catholic Bishops Conference of the Philippines (CBCP), which depicts them as misguided attempts at blindly mimicking Christ that go too far in actualizing his corporeal ordeal. Theologically speaking, ritual nailing is officially proclaimed to manifest a soteriological redundancy—that there should be no reason to subject oneself to physical pain because the necessity for doing so has already been nullified by Christ's ultimate sacrifice. This redundancy, in turn, fuels a popular discourse, prevalent in the Philippines and beyond, that depicts the likes of Jackson as "radical" or "fanatic" representatives of "folk" piety. And while no one, clerical or lay, would intend a personal attack on the character of ritual practitioners, it is ironic that there is great symbolic violence in the comments and questions that are most commonly asked to understand their motivations: how can these people claim to be "good Christians" when they are so misguided in their interpretation of the "Way of the Cross"? How could they possibly think that literally experiencing Christ's pain is the right way of being pious Roman Catholics?

In this book, I will show that an understanding of the motivations that drive these rituals cannot be reduced to a biomedical conception of pain, or measured against prevailing notions of Christian propriety. Instead, the reasons people conduct these rituals are intertwined with very specific and often complex personal intentions, which are as diverse as the individual life circumstances of each practitioner. In seeking to encapsulate the spirit of this diversity, we must first acknowledge a more locally embedded notion of pain, one that is not limited to a state of physical sensation. According to Jackson, whose ideas are echoed by other ritual practitioners in the region, pain (*sakit*) is conceived of as a tribulation "in and of the interior" (*sakit ning lub*). It is from this notion of pain that I posit the idea of "suffering selfhood" that is a central concept of this ethnography. In the context of Passion rituals, suffering is an ontological condition that encompasses a wider spectrum of human hardship beyond forms of strictly corporeal sensation and affect, evoking the states of affliction, misfortune, and misadventure that are encountered in the course of one's life. For sakit to be "maginhawa" refers not to the muting of the physical pain experienced at the point of nailing but to the alleviation of certain aspects of the ritual protagonist's general life predicament, especially in ways that result from God's positive intervention. I submit that we need to see the ritual manifestation of the "Way of the Cross" in terms of this wider, ontological notion of suffering, paying attention to how it is understood as the precondition, rationale, and methodology for pious subject formation in Pampanga.

Ethnographic research for this book was conducted in Pampanga, mainly from 2010 to 2016, using as mediums of interaction the local vernacular Kapampangan and the national language of Filipino.[1] I draw upon in-depth and often exclusive interview data with a host of local stakeholders—including ritual practitioners, clerics, scholars, and government officials. I also draw insight from my own involvement as one of the very few non-Kapampangans in the history of Passion rituals to have been granted a role in the Passion play that frames the nailing events. I place great importance on the perspectives of my local interlocutors, and as such I have attempted to weave the interviews seamlessly into the scholarly analysis. On this note, it is worth pointing out that anthropological ideal of vernacular authenticity is problematized by the tendency of most Kapampangans to linguistically code-switch between Kapampangan and Tagalog, whether in deference to my own linguistic awkwardness or for other reasons. As such, Filipino/Tagalog was most often preferred by my research interlocutors, following reassurances that they were just as able to describe their emotions and understandings of the world in that idiom. I am aware, of course, that conversing in Tagalog opens up a unique milieu of conceptualization. However, I have found it advantageous, both from an analytical and logistical perspective, to simply let those I engaged with speak in the idiom that they deem appropriate. Nevertheless, where I encounter a crucial concept, such as religious or moral-philosophical explanations of ritual behavior, I have requested that my interlocutors "think" and express it Kapampangan.

I consider the insight I gained from various ethnographic encounters alongside an archival examination of primary and secondary sources, paying particular attention to previously unpublished, locally produced oral historical accounts, and a survey of relevant media coverage over the last half-century. My objective in doing so is to describe the ways in which Passion rituals unfold as embodiments of certain historically contingent ideological inheritances, driven and sustained not by the desire for literalism or transcendence but by locally embedded human sensibilities of bereavement, empathy, and trust, their dynamism influenced by institutional forces of Church and State, which occasion agent-driven reinterpretations of what it means to go through hardship and sacrifice. In centralizing how suffering selfhood is the normative basis of *positive* pious agency, I seek to offer insight not only into how ritual pain can be endurable, cathartic, or even desirable but also how suffering selfhood constitutes the devotional context in which Filipino Roman Catholics experience the depth of God's involvement in their lives.

Pampanga's Religious Landscape

The Passion rituals that are the subject of this ethnography unfold in a country that is a testament to the success of Christian missionization in the Far East.[2] Today, over 90 percent of Filipinos are Christian, and 76.18 million (or 80.58 percent of the population) of these are Roman Catholic. This figure from 2013 is an approximately 8 percent increase over the numbers as reported in the Filipino Catholic Directory in 2012 (Uy 2013). The province of Pampanga,[3] which is within the region of central Luzon (region 3), has about 9 percent of the Philippines' total Roman Catholic population, according to the CPCP Catholic Directory released in 2010–2011.[4] Central Luzon has the highest number of Parish churches in the Philippines, 368, a distinction indicated as far back as the first Philippine census in 1903, testifying to the scale and intensity of missionization there beginning in the sixteenth century (Larkin 1972, 13; CBCP 2010–2011).

In the Spanish colonial period, the Pampanga region became among the richest in the colony as a fertile source of agriculture, fishery, and forestry produce, as well both skilled and unskilled labor supporting the growth of other emerging centers, including Manila. Historically, the province of Pampanga stands out as an exemplar of Roman Catholic missionary work, which began in earnest in the latter 1500s. The historian John Leddy Phelan ([1959] 2011) has argued that religious missionization in the province was the most successful in the Philippines, led in significant measure by the pioneering work of the Augustinian order from around 1565. Augustinian Friar Juan de Medina, writing in 1630, observed that the people there "have accepted Christianity more readily than others in the [Philippine] islands" (Medina [1630] 1893, 244; quoted in Larkin 1972, 33). By the middle of the 1600s, "almost all of the natives came under the sway of the Catholic Church" (Larkin 1972, 23).

So successful was missionization in the provincial enclaves of Bacolor and Mexico, for example, that the two priests in charge, F. Lorenzo Barrela and F. Alejandro Dominguez, could hardly cope with the increasing scale of their pastoral duties. By August 1754, the governor-general Pedro Manuel de Arandia granted a petition to create a new middle-of-the-road town as a way to address the burgeoning convert population. These were the circumstances that led to the establishment of what is now the capital city of the province and primary location of this ethnography, San Fernando, which was named after the saintly King of Castile, Fernando Rey. The rituals that we observe in this book, therefore, are performed in towns and villages that are a testament to the literally overflowing success of Roman Catholic penetration.

Conversion to the faith continued in Pampanga through subsequent centuries. Kapampangans were, as historian Luciano Santiago put it, "the trailblazers of the Church, both triumphant and suffering, wounded and healing, and they reflected the religious character and vigor of the faithful" (Santiago 2002, xviii). Kapampangan men and women were among the first to hold respected and important positions in the Church, including the first founders of religious chaplaincies (1592–1699), the first Filipino nuns (1633 and 1636), the first Filipinos ordained to the priesthood (1654 and 1698), the first founders of a native priestly clan (1698–1714), the first Filipino parish priest (1703), the first Filipino native missionary priest and chaplain (1703), the first Filipino vicar general (1741), and the first Filipino doctor in ecclesiastical sciences (1772) (Santiago 2002).

For most of the 1800s, "most of the residents of the province nominally identified themselves as Roman Catholics, even if they did not attend mass regularly" (Larkin 1972, 99). Although there were some significant challenges to the primacy of the Church in the first quarter of the 1900s, particularly from Aglipayan and Protestant Churches, John A. Larkin assessed them as relatively minor (Larkin 1972, 180–181). In the twentieth century, Catholicism was still the dominant religion, with the 1918 official census indicating that about 95 percent of the population belonged to the Church (Villamor and Buencamino 1920, 2:106, 2:394–395).

But this is only one side of the story. Shifting our focus back to the seventeenth century, Friar Medina had also observed that converts from Pampanga "have more to do with Spaniards than the others and try to imitate them as far as possible. But the more they try to do that, the more do *they show their texture as Indians*" (Medina [1630] 1893, 244; Larkin 1972, 33, emphasis mine). Medina's words suggest that in spite of the enthusiasm with which most in Pampanga took to the faith, and regardless of the extent to which Kapampangan converts had "more to do with the Spaniards," they still did not quite qualify as "real" members of the community of faithful. It was as though their vehement acceptance of Christianity was illegitimate because it was based on a form of acquisition that, in spite of their good intentions, testified to the enduring tenacity of their preexisting belief systems. Medina's observations, applicable just as much in the seventeenth century as they are today, are a typical example of missionary frustration at the failure to eradicate all traces of indigenous religiosity amid the sustained effort at liturgical and doctrinal inculcation. In spite of quantitative success in conversion, and in spite of the outward, pioneering show of doctrinal and liturgical adherence by Kapampangans, there remains a sense that the missionary endeavor is far from complete. None had personified this more than Kapampangans such as Felipe Salvador, known as Apu Ipe, the supreme pontiff of the Santa Iglesia who was excommunicated by the Roman Catholic Church and convicted of sedition by the American authorities for threatening the public order (Larkin 1972, 237). As scholars such as historian Reynaldo Ileto (1979) have observed, shamans, folk healers, and sectarian preachers in this region were very influential as leaders because they tapped into the wellsprings of certain indigenous notions of brotherhood and inner fortitude that presented significant challenges to the colonial order. Their influence, in spite of their limited success, testified to the possibility that the local "texture as Indians" would manifest itself in something different, perhaps illicit, from what missionaries and colonial administrators had originally intended.

The complexity of social and religious development continue to manifest in ritual practice in contemporary Kapampangan society. One of the most common things that I have been told in the course of my research in Pampanga is that the province "splits in two" during Holy Week. On one side of the split—typically associated with the middle class and provincial elite—Roman Catholics from around the province pursue ritual acts with strong emphasis on sacramental and liturgical participation. Attendance at Holy Mass would typically be followed by participating in Parish-sponsored community events such as the Visita Iglesia, a family or group pilgrimage to a number of churches around the province. Another popular activity during Holy Week is the procession and public displaying of family-owned antique statuary, which are wheeled around the parish vicinity in motorized illuminated floats with elaborate floral arrangements. In these processional parades, high-status members of the social elite see Holy Week as an opportunity to reiterate their family's historical commitment to shared religious values, and also their inheritance of a lineage of missionization (Castro 2007b).

The other side of the split, meanwhile, "prefers festivity to solemnity" in celebrating Holy Week through paraliturgical gatherings. This is the world of the pain-inflicting ritual agent, one that cultural commentator Robby Tantingco has described as "a parallel universe where God dwells not in the Tabernacle but in the [makeshift chapels], where His Word can be found not in the Scripture but in the [vernacular scripture] pasyon, and where His forgiveness can be obtained not in the sacrament of Penance but in extreme penitence like whipping your back and carrying your literal cross" (Tantingco 2010a). The activities in this realm of "popular" religious piety carry with them connotations of the carnivalesque wherein, as the anthropologist Nicholas Barker described it, "the sacred and profane often co-exist harmoniously. . . . Celebration and mourning are not regarded as mutually exclusive or ritually incompatible. On Good Friday, clad in loincloths, the Kristos were crucified to the backdrop of a big-dipper" (Barker 1998, 19). The anthropologist Peter Bräunlein (2009, 908–909) likewise describes the religious landscape in the region as "comparable to a thrilling circus performance or public executions during early modern times in Europe."

It may well be the case that those with proselytizing mandates would consider the split nature of Catholicism in Pampanga as a "failure of missionization." The point I seek to make here, however, is not that religion in Pampanga falls short of a missionizing ideal. Rather, it is important to underscore that people in Pampanga are not completely and unquestioningly beholden to the rich legacy bestowed by colonial and religious institutions in pursuit of their relationship with God. Revealing their "texture as Indians" means that people in the region embody their religious inheritance in ways that are meaningful to their individual life circumstances, even if this involves challenging and reinterpreting the most central tenets of the faith, such as how one is to pursue the "Way of the Cross."

Rather than harking to a hopelessly immutable ontology, what we may discover as the ethnographic encounter of this book unfolds is that the suffering selfhoods that are crafted in the performance of Passion rituals is an aspect of the cultivation of personhood in the here and now. This is to say that the transcendental and soteriological outcomes that are conventionally associated with Christian ritual suffering are instead reoriented to be coterminous with aspirations in "everyday" life, even in contexts outside formalized worship. Contemporary pious agency, then, describes the set of practices that are meaningful because they provide people with the moral, ethical, and sentimental wellsprings from which to draw as they face the vicissitudes and ruptures of modernity.

This ethnography follows from and builds upon previous anthropological research on religious rituals in the central Luzon region.[5] I have structured this book around three distinct thematic currents, namely: ideologies, investments, and institutions. Each of these themes explores different aspects of how the ideal of suffering encourages forms of ritual embodiment. In the following sections, I provide a summary of the rationale behind each theme, outlining how each chapter of the book elaborates upon it, and a brief account of the scholarly and disciplinary currents from which I draw and to which, in turn, I seek to contribute.

Ideologies

The first thematic current of this book is a critical ontology of "suffering selfhood." This primarily involves an analytical reflexivity about the contingent historical, cultural, and doctrinal forces that operated to constitute a particular kind of pious Christian subjectivity. The basic questions here are: How did the idea that "suffering is good" come about as a central concept in the formation of Christian selfhoods? And how were these ideologies channeled into ritual practice in the early Christian Church and beyond? The work of critical theorist Michel Foucault is valuable as a methodological influence in this regard. It is from his exploration of themes such as disciplinarity, governmentality, power, corporeality, and biopolitics that we learn to apply genealogical investigations of ideas to examining how "the self" is constituted, particularly in a Christian context (Besley 2005, 377). In the first part of chapter 1, as such, I discuss an ideological and discursive shift that occurred as far back as the second century, in which the Christian relationship with suffering became reversed from something to be avoided to an experience that can liberate both the body and the soul. I focus on how the growing discursive currency of this kind of "good" suffering selfhood made it possible to equate the persecuted martyrdom of Christ's early followers with the performance of acts and rites of radical asceticism—collectively known as *disciplina*—particularly in the medieval monastery in various parts of Europe. These acts were premised on the stipulation that the body must be purified through pain, thereby purging it of its impulses toward sin and transgression, and orienting its practitioner toward achieving spiritual transcendence as promised by God.

In the second part of chapter 1, I move on to discuss how this ideology of suffering selfhood formed the basis for the practice of rituals of ascetic self-mortification. I trace the proliferation of lay flagellant brotherhoods across Europe, and later still, the adoption of rites of self-mortification as part of an ensemble of missionary strategies deployed in the Christianization of New World and beyond. In the Philippines, I show that acts of disciplina were introduced by Spanish missionaries as early as the sixteenth century—either as flagellation, or other forms of self-inflicted pain—as way of cultivating the normativity of suffering selfhood as a means of atonement among converted lowland populations.

To gain a full appreciation of these themes, it would not suffice to simply recall the archival incidence of Passion rituals in the Philippines. Since the suffering selfhood channeled in Passion rituals evokes a central, fundamental tenet of the Christian faith, I have found it necessary to draw upon the fields of classics, particularly works such as those of Caroline Walker Bynum (1987), Judith Perkins (1995) and Werner Jaeger (1985), who have discussed the ideological significance of corporeality and how it formed the basis for the Christian Church's social, political, and institutional development. In addition to this, I have drawn from the work of cultural critics, especially Michel Foucault (1986, 1997a, 1997b) and Talal Asad (1973, 1993), who have made strong arguments about how the regulation of bodies, whether through formal institutions or individual volition, have greatly influenced the ideological and discursive formations that condition modern societies (especially Christian ones). This theme is, in short, an ideological history on which an understanding of the contemporary local, corporeal manifestations of Christian suffering is framed in Pampanga.

Investments

Whereas the first theme explored the historicity of the ideology of suffering, in the second thematic movement I shift the focus to the ethnographic present. In a cluster of three chapters, I emphasize how Passion rituals in Pampanga are motivated by emotional and sentimental investments made in pursuit of reciprocal relationships with God. They are "investments" because ritual action is premised, at least in part, on the hope that God would respond favorably to painful ritual acts with a benefit that would apply in their lifetimes rather than as a deferred benefit in the afterlife. As such, Passion rituals evoke culturally resonant notions of empathy, trust, and bereavement, notions that condition the form and substance of ritual action during Holy Week. I seek in these three chapters to situate the ethnography of suffering more firmly into a phenomenological anthropology of the body. In so doing, I provide empirical substance to the notion that the living body is the canvas on which our relationships with others are transacted and cultivated toward the formation of specific kinds of pious personhoods. Collectively, the chapters in this section contribute to an interdisciplinary discussion about rituals of the body-in-pain, for example, in the works of anthropologists Elizabeth Collins (1997) on Thaipusam rituals in Malaysia, Margaret Chan (2006) on Tang Ki rituals in Singapore, James Laidlaw (1995) on Jain renouncers in India, and David Pinault (1993) on Shia Lamentation rituals in India.

In chapter 2, I focus on the pious acts derived from the reading and chanting of the *pasyon:* vernacular religious texts that emphasized the redemptive and salvific value of suffering. I consider not just the impact of the pasyon but of its vocally projected version: a ritual called pabasa. In this ritual, the faithful come together for long hours of the day and night to chant the Passion story and, in so doing, identify with each other in bereavement of the crucified Christ. I argue that the chanting of the pabasa triggers a form of emotional contagion of bereavement and pity— one that could be called a "sonic piety"—that not only cultivates specific pious subjectivities for the pasyon chanter but also conditions a distinctive aural landscape in Pampanga in which other painfully embodied Passion rituals become meaningful.

In elaborating on the pasyon and pabasa, I seek to add ethnographic nuance to the most prominent tradition of Filipino historiographical works that examine how popular religious piety led to the production of subaltern subjects, particularly at the ruptures of colonial society. Historians Reynaldo Ileto (1979), John D. Blanco (2009), Filomeno Aguilar (1998), and Vicente Rafael (1988) have, in reiterating the importance of subaltern agency, heightened our understanding of how Catholicism was subject to processes of local resistance and reinterpretation. Scholars such as Joseph Scalice (2009), anthropologist Robert Love (2004), and political theorist Benedict Anderson (quoted in Love 2004), meanwhile, have called for a need to imbue these otherwise exemplary historiographical works with the synchronic depth of ethnographic analysis. In this second chapter, I do just that by bringing the historical discourse into productive conversation with the anthropology of sensation (specifically, aural), in which analytical attention is placed on how embodied experience and subjectivity are conditioned by sonic environments under historically and culturally changing circumstances. In this regard, this second thematic movement is characterized by my effort to bring historians of the Philippines in conversation with anthropologists of the body, particularly those who have more recently written about the sensual aspects of sound and aurality, such as anthropologists Steven Feld (1990, 1996), Tim Ingold (2011), Nathan Porath (2008), and Charles Hirschkind (2006) to name just a few.

In chapter 3, I focus on pagdarame, or ritual self-flagellation as a form of embodied ritual investment. The starting point for this is to challenge the widely held assumption, the historicity of which I explored in chapter 1, that self-flagellation is exclusively coterminous with the desire to atone for one's sins. While flagellation might at times be referred to as *"penitensya"* (penitence), what ritual practitioners emphasize as central in their ritual investment is *"darame,"* both a feeling of and acting out of empathy. I show that the empathy that is crafted in pagdarame goes beyond a two-way vicarious identification with Christ's Passion experience. As an embodiment of suffering selfhood, I argue that self-flagellation is a triangulated empathy, whereby an intersubjective link is formed between God, the flagellant, and a particular person for whose benefit God's positive intervention is sought. By focusing on self-flagellation as a triangulated empathy, I seek to make a contribution to a debate about the nature in empathic intersubjectivity that, as anthropologists Douglas Hollan and C. Jason Throop (2011) observe, calls fourth some of the most important discussions from the fields of philosophy, history, and the social sciences about the possibility for gaining epistemological access to the experience of others. I provide ethnographic specificity to the position that empathy is entwined with a web of related concepts, including pity, fellow feeling and emotional contagion. I further seek to add to related scholarship that has dealt with the theme of local articulations of moral and religious concepts, including the works of anthropologists John McAndrew (2001),

Fenella Cannell (1999), Robert Love (2004), and Raul Pertierra (1988); sociologists such as Jayeel Cornelio (2016); theatre studies scholars such as William Peterson (2016) and Sir Anril Tiatco (2016); and historians such as Deirdre de la Cruz (2015).

I further expand on the theme of ritual investments in chapter 4, where I focus on acts of ritual nailing, pamamaku king krus, both as a theatrical performance and as a ritual of divine vow fulfillment. I describe the institutional history of the ritual from the 1950s and comment upon the political, social, and economic conditions that make the ritual possible. As far as the declared motivations of namamaku (nailees) are concerned, the central premise given is that nailing is a form of *"panata,"* a term that describes a promise or a vow made to God in response to, or appealing for, his positive intervention into the life of the ritual practitioner. I describe how namamaku reconceptualize pain as spiritually edifying of their personal relationships with other ritual protagonists, with whom bonds of trust (*tiuala ya lub*) are formed. Following this discussion, I convey a sense of my wider ethnographic encounters with namamaku—particularly female ritual protagonists—outside of the main theatrical context of the ritual.

Chapter 4 contributes a critical tenor to the longstanding anthropological concern with determining not just what ritual is about but also what it is for. Scholars in the subfield of ritual studies have carried anthropology's conceptualizations, classifying the "effect" of ritual (or, to cite Seligman et al. [2008], ritual's "consequences") as bifurcated along a dichotomy promulgated in the structural-functionalism of sociologist Talcott Parsons (1951): between the "instrumental," goal-oriented aspects on the one hand, and on the other the representational, "expressive/symbolic" aspect of formalism that has no "real" ends other than to depict and exemplify hidden realities or subjunctive scenarios. This is a discourse summed up by William Sturman Sax, Johannes Quack, and Jan Weinhold (2010), who argue that if scholars see ritual as "a problem," it is so not because the motivations of its protagonists are irrational or nonsensical but because ritual action is ineffective in achieving any practical, operational efficacies. Arguing against this disciplinary fixation on ritual efficacy, I draw from performance studies to examine not just what Passion rituals do but the kinds of subjectivities and agencies that are cultivated in the process of conducting it. In chapter 4, I take on topics such as: how ritual intentions are embodied through theatrical performance; how ritual vows are fulfilled through the cultivation of the body's capacity to withstand pain; how bonds of intersubjective trust among ritual protagonists are formed in the pursuit of embodied rituals.

Institutions

I direct the discussion of ritual investments outward toward a third main theme, which is a consideration of how institutional, political, and economic forces condition understandings and enactments of suffering selfhoods. Although the Passion rituals are extraliturgical in their practice, as I demonstrate particularly in chapters 3 and 4, the main point I make in the last two chapters is that the role of the Roman Catholic Church and the Philippine State are influential factors that condition pious agency and social personhood, especially when it extends beyond the ritual domains of Pampanga. This analytical shift is resonant with anthropologists Akhil Gupta and James Ferguson's (1992, 40) observations that religious subjectivities are not only determined or mediated by the interplay of doctrines, traditions, and customs but are also subject to the vicissitudes of "political, economic determinations that have a logic of their own." In light of this, I expand the analytical breadth beyond the embodied ritual suffering by focusing on what anthropologists Veena Das, Arthur Kleinman, and Margaret M. Lock (1997, 2) have described as "the collective and individual human suffering associated with life conditions shaped by powerful social forces." In these chapters I reiterate more firmly that pious agency is conditioned by institutional powers, particularly as ritual agents seek material upliftment outside of the ritual sphere.

In chapter 5, I discuss the dynamics of official institutional Church policies as they pertain to Passion rituals. This discussion is framed against the more general question, how does the Church as an influential institution condition the continued practice of Passion rituals, and by extension, Christian subjectivity? There are two aspects to this discussion. First, I examine those discourses of official clerical disavowal of Passion rituals as "wrong," "illicit," and even "fanatic." One way to do this is to trace what it is, exactly, that makes Passion rituals problematic from a theological and doctrinal point of view. While I do not aim at a theological exegesis here, I do seek to convey the critical tenor of Church pronouncements about Passion rituals. Following that, I turn the discussion toward more informal discursive spaces and practices among the clergy themselves, through which can be observed the diversity, or in some instances the reversal, of official clerical opinions "on the ground." The emphasis here is on the sentimental spaces and practices among clergy themselves as facets of a theologically "incultured" approach to ritual investments in Pampanga.

The discussion in chapter 5 aligns with a robust body of scholarship from clerical orders, particularly in the fields of philosophy and psychology. The orientation of these works has been on two fronts: first, the persistence of, in the words of Jesuit scholar Jaime Bulatao (1966), a "split-level" Catholicism as a symptom of a psychopathological malaise of Filipino Catholics, one that can be corrected by spiritual guidance and theological instruction. Second, this chapter contributes to a discussion of inculturation, which is a set of theologically based precepts in which Roman Catholic doctrine is made to coincide with indigenous belief. This has led to examinations of the works of scholar-clerics such as Leonardo Mercado,

SJ; Dionisio Miranda, SVD; Albert Alejo, SJ; and Jaime Bulatao, SJ. While the conceptual leanings of this chapter are aligned more toward anthropology than theology, I write it in a way that is responsive to the call for a closer collaboration between those two disciplines as emphasized in the works of theologians Francis Clooney (2010), Albertus Bagus Laksana (2014), and anthropologists Philip Fountain and Sin Wen Lau (2013).

In chapter 6, I situate the ideology and normativity of suffering within the role of the state bureaucracy in co-opting notions of suffering and sacrifice toward certain political and economic agendas. The focus is on how the positive value of suffering, a sentiment so crucial in Passion rituals, has become discursively appropriated and operationalized by formal institutions as part of a mandate of deploying economically productive overseas workers. I show how certain ideas of suffering are invoked by politicians and state agencies through tropes of "hero martyrism" and "suffering missionaries," and through which overseas Filipino workers (OFWs) are encouraged to associate the nation's well-being as an extension of their own pursuit of personal well-being.

This discussion resonates with scholarly works that have discussed the religiously inflected hero martyrism of OFWs by analyzing how their experiences are conditioned by specific ideological notions of race and gender (Aguilar et al. 2009; Choy 2003; Constable 2007; Guevarra 2010; S. McKay 2011; Ong 2006; Parreñas 2008; Pertierra 1988; and Tyner 2000). Other works have highlighted the process in which state policies on labor migration craft, or even compel, specific commitments to the nation (Franco 2011; Hau 2004; Rodriguez 2006; Tadiar 2009). Relatively fewer works have gone into great detail about how the Filipino transnational economy is a domain for the expression and deployment of religious agency, particularly among men. My discussion along these lines addresses a crucial need to add to two analytical currents in particular: scholars such as Kale Bantigue Fajardo (2011), Steven McKay (2011), and Alicia Pinggol (2001) have generated momentum in the analysis of the "masculinization" of OFW heroism, while Filomeno Aguilar (1999), Mark Johnson and Pnina Werbner (2010), and Mario Lopez (2012) have considered the OFW experience with respect to the affective and religious aspects that condition the workers' socioeconomic motivations. Both chapters address the idea that personhood is not simply subject to forms of domination and hierarchy from institutions such as the state and the Church. Modern subjecthood and well-being, rather, is cultivated by those whose suffering is part of an ensemble of strategies that seek to create or remake themselves as self-conscious agents in the world.

PART I

Ideologies

The Ideology of Suffering in Medieval and Colonial Domains

When asking about the history of Roman Catholic Passion rituals in the Philippines, one is confronted with an empirical conundrum. On the one hand, the colonial archival record shows that painful religious rituals in the Philippines were introduced and encouraged by Spanish missionaries as early as four centuries ago. On the other hand, one would be hard-pressed to find a practitioner of Passion rituals today who would intuitively think of his or her religious practice as a direct inheritance from the colonial period. Tonette Orejas, a journalist who has been covering religious life in Pampanga for many decades, echoes the general consensus that I have come across in studying Holy Week rituals in central Luzon: "No one could say exactly when [rituals of self-flagellation] actually started," she writes. "The usual reply was, *'akagisnan mi namu ini'* [this was already in practice when we were growing up]" (Orejas 2010). The challenge that confronts us in this chapter is how to come to terms with a certain incongruity, one in which the historical record of Passion rituals does not always match, and at times seems at odds with, the anthropological "thickness" we encounter from speaking to practitioners themselves.

Take, for example, my conversation with Lito Santos, a man from the city of San Fernando, who has been conducting rituals of self-flagellation for "at least twenty years." He explained the origins of his practice of self-flagellation by telling me a story from his youth. In January 1995, Lito was among the millions of Filipinos who gathered at Manila's Luneta Park to celebrate Pope John Paul II's visit to the Philippines. Lito had managed to get a glimpse of His Holiness as he delivered his address: "When I heard the Santo Papa speak about honoring my parents," he said, "I realized that I needed to devote my own suffering to help them. . . . God favors those who suffer for something good." Taking up the Pope's example meant following a fairly prevalent family tradition. He continued, "I heard that Santo Papa himself does [flagellation]. So I decided to do it myself. My family is not that religious, [but] a few of my uncles and some friends read and chant the pasyon. Normally they do flagellation because they feel a sense of heaviness inside of them [*mabigat ang loob*]."

Lito's story points to a widely held Filipino responsiveness to the words and deeds of revered figures of Roman Catholicism, as well as to the pious practices of close friends and relatives. Instead of identifying with an Iberian colonial history, Lito considered his ritual agency as derived from his membership in what could be called, to evoke the classicist Judith Perkins, a virtuous "community of sufferers" (Perkins 1995, 200). What the members of this community have in common is a conviction in a positive correlation between the body-in-pain and the prospect of divine favor. After all, Lito found in the Pope not just a revered leader of the Church but also a fellow sufferer who embodied a fundamental tenet of Christianity: "God favors those who suffer for something good."

Statements about the positive value of suffering are not at all out of the ordinary among Filipino Roman Catholics. A survey conducted by Verbite scholar Benigno Beltran of about ten thousand respondents found that the image that most Filipinos identified with was that of the suffering Christ (Beltran 1987, 38). In displacing direct colonial inheritance as the primary basis for a positive attitude toward suffering, however, Lito and practically all self-flagellants in Pampanga encourage the pursuit of a more nuanced historicity in our attempts to understand the precursors of Passion rituals. As anthropologist Michel-Rolf Trouillot (1995, 22–29) has defined it, "historicity" is a way of engaging with the past that correlates the process of archival research with people's "narrative constructions about that process." But more than adopting an expanded empirical range, I align this historicity toward considering how discursive formations—particularly those ideologies that underscore the importance of rituals of pain—intersect with "the operations and felt immediacies of bodies" (Scheper-Hughes 1995; Hollan and Throop 2011). As such, this chapter is one that combines a historiography of ideas with an anthropology of corporeality and embodiment. We shall proceed along two analytical threads:

First, I nuance the discussion of exemplary religious role models by first asking fundamental questions about the ideological normativity of "suffering," and how it came to be thought of as coterminous with the practical cultivation of pious Christian virtue. How did suffering, at least in a religious sense, become positively conceived in Christianity? Under what discursive circumstances did an equivalency between self-inflicted pain and religious piety occur? In pursuing these questions, I devote the first section to a discussion of the ideological legacy of "suffering selfhood," including a brief examination of the ideals of early Christian martyrs as well as the development of the Christian movement from its Greco-Roman inheritances.[1] I show how the ideal of Christian martyrdom became channeled toward a repertoire of corporeal techniques of pain infliction—collectively known as *disciplina*—which in turn facilitated the pursuit of spiritual deliverance that characterizes "suffering selfhood." The second objective of this chapter is to discuss the conditions under which the physical embodiment of suffering selfhood became transmitted to a Philippine context, focusing on how rituals of self-inflicted pain were introduced in the Philippines by various missionary orders as modes of seeking atonement and pursuing divine reconciliation. An examination along these lines will lay the foundation for an understanding of how self-flagellation became a defining characteristic of the kind of virtuous exemplars such as the Pope that Lito and many other people in Pampanga relate to so strongly.

The Positive Value of Suffering

Lito's suggestion that the Pontiffs engaged in self-flagellation is not at all far-fetched. Monsignor Slawomir Oder, the biographer of Pope John Paul II, observed that the latter always had in his bedroom "an unusual trouser belt that he used as a whip and always brought to Castel Gandolfo" (Oder and Gaeta 2010). In flagellating himself, John Paul II was enacting a recurrent theme in his own theological exegesis, which has emphasized a link between embodying Christ's suffering and the cultivation of particular kinds of pious dispositions, namely atonement, redemption, and communion.[2] This was a link in which his predecessor, Pope John XXIII, likewise believed. The latter said that self-inflicted pain was the best way of commemorating the great monastics of the Church who, "pure as they were[,] . . . inflicted such mortifications upon themselves as to leave us almost aghast with admiration." Contemplation of these pious exemplars meant that the faithful ought to be "moved by God's grace to impose on ourselves some voluntary sufferings and deprivations" (Pope John XXIII 1962).

The positive value of suffering is fundamental to the development of Roman Catholicism itself. If we look even further back in the history of the Church, the normativity of the body-in-pain can be linked to a rein-terpretation of Christ's death, one influenced by the increasing preva-lence of hagiographies of martyr acts from the fourth century. The idea of martyrdom that was represented in the Apocryphal Acts of the Apostles extolled a new ideological premise that suggested that the body was not obliterated by the Roman Empire's punitive regime. From being viewed as vulnerable, perpetually harassed, and tormented, the martyr's suffer-ing body came to be seen as a virtuous and victorious one in the mold of Jesus himself. The essence of the "Jesus movement" was that representa-tions of bodily pain and suffering encouraged the cultivation of a new subjectivity of the human person—that of the "self as sufferer" (Perkins 1995, 246). Suffering, in particular, self-punishment, was seen as provid-ing an opportunity for transcendence: "In such piety, the body is not so much a hindrance to the soul's ascent as the opportunity for it" observes Medieval historian Catherine Walker Bynum, who described the suffer-ing body as manifesting a "physicality [that] was not to be eradicated since this flesh could be merged with that flesh whose agony, espoused by choice, was salvation" (Bynum 1987, 246; see also Mellor 1991, 57).

The history of the Roman Catholic Church is replete with examples of individuals who, inspired by the suffering of Jesus, have willfully "mortified" themselves.[3] In the Christian tradition, "mortification" connotes a "putting the flesh to death," which in turn involves the voluntary infliction of pain upon one's body as part of a process of sanctification. "If you live after the flesh you shall die," says the apostle Paul, "but if through the spirit you mortify the deeds of the flesh, you shall live" (Romans 8:13; Galatians 5:24).[4] The saints were virtuous not because of their feats of superhuman pain endurance. They were saints because they were mentally, physically, and emotionally conditioned to embody a certain transcendental truth about the spirit, a truth that reiterated the emphasis on the body's salvific potential.

Yet in a very important way, the saintly exemplars, including Pope John Paul II, personified a fundamental paradox of the Christian faith. Anthropologists Maya Mayblin and Magnus Course (2014, 312) have observed that while Christ's ultimate self-sacrifice expunges the need for any direct or actual enactment of suffering, Christianity's soteriological mandate nevertheless exacts that all subsequent pious human actions must still enact that sacrifice in some physical form. Theatre historian Friedman Kreuder (2008, 181) acknowledges the centrality of the literal imitation of Christ in this paradox. In his analysis of medieval Passion plays and flagellation practices, Kreuder observed that "the aspiration was "not merely to have faith but to be in fact an image of Christ . . . literally embodied during the performance of flagellation." The pursuit of imitating Christ required a regimented program of disciplinary acts and practices. In this sense, mortification could be seen as not just a way of acquiring religious knowledge but as an active, embodied form of discipline, particularly in monastic institutions. It is to the implementation of this form of corporeal practice in medieval Christian institutions that we shall now turn.

Disciplina: The Punitive Economy of the Christian Body

As much as the ideal of cultivating suffering selfhood is intertwined with the story of the early Christian martyrs, its institutionalization as a ritual practice evokes the lineage of the Hellenization of Christianity. As classicist Werner Jaeger (1985) points out, Greek saint's lives produced the models for the ideological normativity of suffering subjecthood that would form the basis for Christianity's continued institutional growth. The formation and transformation of the pious Christian subject, however, depended on more than just the capacity to imagine, perceive, and imitate martyric exemplars. Christians had adopted and modified practices of self-cultivation from ancient Greek philosophy in the refinement of forms of ritual embodiment. In this context, there are two Greek concepts that are relevant.

First, Christian subject formation drew inspiration from notions such as *paideia*, which refers to the suite of educational and self-cultivating practices adopted for the purposes of enhancing a person's physical, intellectual, and moral subjectivities in the Greek cosmopolis (Jaeger 1985). Moreover, Christian subject formation drew on the notion of *askēsis*, literally "training," from which is derived the term "asceticism." Askēsis is a proactive deployment of corporeal acts designed to reiterate the centrality of the body in the pursuit of transcendence. In Michel Foucault's definition, askēsis was part of "technologies of the self" that aimed at the self-initiated transformation of subjectivity as the basis for the achievement of profound transcendence. Foucault emphasized that askēsis involved more than just physical exertion but also an inward-focused set of practices aimed at self-care, including the cultivation of one's relationship with truth. It is then that askēsis contributed toward a "full, perfect, and complete relationship of oneself to oneself" (Foucault 2001, 320). In channeling askēsis, one engages in a positive acquisition of skills and sensibilities that are conducted "to effect by their own means, or with the help of others, a certain number of operations on their own bodies and souls, thoughts, conduct, and way of being, so as to transform themselves in order to attain a certain state of happiness, purity, wisdom, perfection, or immortality" (Foucault 1997a, 225).

In the specific context of Christian self-formation, the anthropologist Talal Asad (1987, 168) has associated askēsis with a punitive economy of the Christian body, in which the embodied cultivation of askēsis involved "a strong sense of chastisement, correction, and the penalty inflicted for a fault." The embodiment of askēsis, therefore, was conducted in the context of what Asad (1983, 314) describes as a "community of those who stand with him as sinners before God."

In the history of Roman Catholicism, the programmatic, regimented inculcation of askēsis as an economy of the body was fundamental to the ideas and practices of individuals crucial in the establishment of the Christian monastic institution. A pioneer of this spirit of ascetic self-denial was Saint Benedict (480–550), who prescribed a set of rules and regimented acts that channeled askēsis in strengthening a person's (particularly monks) corporeal and spiritual resolve. "Disciplina" was a term that denoted a range of corporeal practices aimed, as Niklaus Largier (2007, 30) argues, at "the arousal of emotion and imagination" through "rituals that aim to unfetter desire, imagination, and the passions." As Peter van der Veer observed (1995, 367), monastics "had to be disciplined to experience the Christian truth . . . a learning by inconveniences."

Another of the earliest pioneers of this punitive economy of the Christian body was Saint Peter Damian (1007–1072/1073), who Church historian G. J. Cuming (1978, 148) considered "the first great protagonist of voluntary flagellation."[5] In "De Laude Flagellorum" (In praise of flagellation), Damian (1959, 35) specifically reiterated that self-whipping was a commensurate way of channeling the ascetic's sinfulness toward the transcendent aims of Christian subjecthood, declaring, "I scourge both flesh and spirit because I know that I have offended in both flesh and spirit." For Damian, one's spiritual duty did not only reside in sequestering oneself from the world of earthly pleasure through the ascetic numbing of the senses, or through learning about the legacies of martyrdom and sacrifice. Damian encouraged the pursuit of the exemplary model of Jesus, imitatio Christi: "Perfectly to imitate Christ, it is necessary to share His pain; but life does not provide us with such pains as these, and so we must inflict them on ourselves: this is the ascetic" (36). This imitation involved ritual forms of ascetic self-denial, which included "denying aspects of one's self, self-abnegation, self-renunciation; self-discipline or self-control in not gratifying, abstaining or indulging one's desires or impulses, abstinence, asceticism, austerity and also connotations of selflessness and self-sacrifice. In extreme religious forms it may involve mortification of the flesh" (Besley 2005, 377).

Both Saint Damian and Saint Benedict would stipulate that disciplina needed to be regulated by monastic authorities who surveilled and supervised its correct and exact application to the monk's body. Foucault, however, also points to a disciplina that required a regime of self-surveillance and regulation against the body's naturally sinful inclinations. This auto-surveillance, in itself premised upon a suspicion of the unchecked body's innate tendencies, defined the monastic subject's commitment to the ideal of Christian piety. Disciplina, then, was inward-focused, practiced in private, and evoked what sociologists of religion Chris Shilling and Philip Mellor (2010, 531) have called " a collective habitus which can be experienced as liberating and transformative, however shocking it might appear to modern eyes."

Following from the traditions of Saints Benedict and Damian, self-flagellation featured as part the spiritual exercises stipulated by the founder of the Society of Jesus (Jesuits), Ignatius of Loyola, who in 1548 encouraged its practice in both individual and group contexts. The exercises are a set of meditations, prayers, and practices designed to be performed daily and in private over the course of four weeks. They are based on the theological premise that God's will for all mankind can be appreciated through an appeal to the human senses. They are aimed specifically at the physical and psychological training of first-year Jesuit novitiates under the guidance of a spiritual director during seclusion. Self-mortification is conducted as one of the ways of expressing penance for the sins one has committed, in which the faithful are encouraged "to chastise the flesh, that is, giving it sensible pain, which is given by wearing haircloth or cords or iron chains next to the flesh, by scourging or wounding oneself, and by other kinds of austerity" (Loyola 2007, 50–51).

Often the adoption of flagellation by those outside the monastery coincided with events of great natural calamities and social upheaval, and there have been reports in the historical record of flagellant groups gathering in various parts of the Christian world from the fourteenth century onward. By the sixteenth century, flagellant cofradias such as the Vera Cruz in Salamanca even received sanction and benefaction from Pope Julian in 1508, and further legitimacy under Pope Paul III in 1536. The Council of Trent (1545–1563) provided a further boost to the spread of flagellant confraternities, with disciplina seen as an exemplary way of manifesting Tridentine reform (see Carroll 2002). By the mid-seventeenth century in Spain and southern Italy, according to Michael Carroll (2002, 84), "public flagellation meant several different things simultaneously to both Church authorities and to the laity: it was an expression of Christocentric piety, a way of expiating sin and so a way of ending natural and social disasters, and a form of entertainment." Practices of flagellation continued throughout Italy in the early nineteenth century, and in Rome itself it was observed to have been practiced as late as 1870 (Toke 1909). "Through the blows of the lash," argued Largier (2007, 180–181), common folk believed that they could "placate the anger of God, who was threatening to destroy the world in his wrath against the sinfulness of men."

Disciplina continued to be practiced fairly predominantly among various religious orders (Murray 1988).[6] Flagellation, either self-inflicted or received, was a feature of the missionary efforts of two Catholic religious orders in particular: the Society of Jesus (Jesuits) and the Order of Saint Francis (Franciscans). Roman Catholic missionaries from these orders had introduced disciplina as part of their evangelizing missions in the New World in Mexico (Clendinnen 1991, 123–124; J. S. Smith 2000), where flagellant groups such as the Los Hermanos Penitentes are thought to have descended from the Third Order of Saint Francis of Assisi (J. S. Smith 2000, 71). The sociologist of religion Michael Carroll observed that flagellant brotherhood groups, primarily inspired by the Franciscan order, flourished in Mexico City from at least 1527, and in Guadalajara and Zacatecas in 1551, with flagellation groups with as many as seven thousand on Good Friday (Carroll 2002, 81).

The encounter with the mission field connected the missionary with the predicament of the early Church itself, thereby placing clerics in favorable conditions for martyrdom. As Christianity developed and spread institutionally, the ideal of suffering selfhood continued to be a defining feature of the missionary endeavor—that being a missionary in a faraway land, often under the threat of dislocation, misadventure, or death, was itself a form of pious suffering. It is to how flagellation was part of the missionary endeavor in the Philippines that we shall now turn.

Spanish Colonial Missions: Disciplina in the Philippines

Thus far I have described the context in which the ideology of suffering selfhood had been channeled into modes of corporeal ritual agency, and how that process eventually moved out of the medieval monastery to widespread adoption among the laity. In essence, self-inflicted physical suffering was meaningful because it evoked the victorious spirit of the early martyrs, and in that sense evoked the central soteriological truth of Christianity itself. Ritual pain infliction drew inspiration from Greco-Roman concepts of the cultivation of the mind and body. But, as Michel Foucault has argued, the Christian concepts of "asceticism" and "self-denial" are different from their Greco-Roman precedents. Whereas askēsis involved the positive acquisition of something that "does not reduce: it equips, it provides" (Foucault 2001, 320), the modes of Christian asceticism promulgated in the medieval monastery involved the Christian subject's detachment and renunciation from the world (Besley 2005, 373–374).

Spanish Missions in the Philippines did tend to follow the evangelistic strategies employed in Nuevo Mexico (Irving 2010, 113; Balsera 2005). As Carroll (2002, 81) observed, Roman Catholic missionary activities throughout rural Europe and beyond—especially those conducted by the Franciscan and Jesuit orders—were characterized by "a strong penitential emphasis that involved flagellation." As the historian Carolyn Brewer (2004, 70–71) has observed, the practice of flagellation that was spread from Spain to the Philippines "was widely accepted by new converts" as "mainstream religious practice."[7] The main significant point here, however, is that the practice of flagellation that was introduced in the Philippine colonial setting had a strong emphasis on extolling the flagellant to be aware of his own sinfulness and orient himself toward atonement and formal reconciliation with God. Thus, as can be seen from the following section, the common theme among missionary accounts of the practices is what Brewer has called the "dual technology of confession and flagellation" (63).

One of the earliest mentions of flagellation comes from the Jesuit order, the first of which arrived in the Philippines from Mexico in 1581, establishing mission stations in Luzon and the Visayas. Jesuit Pedro Chirino's *Relacion de Las Islas Filipinas*, which detailed "occurrences in Manila in 1596 and 1597," attributed the beginnings of flagellation to the devotion of Canon Diego de Leon in the 1590s, who encouraged "the practice of assembling in our church many men of all ranks to take the discipline [that is, to scourge themselves, as a voluntary presence—a practice then common among religious devotees], three days in the week, especially during Lent." (Chirino, quoted in Blair and Robertson 1903, 12:249) Significantly, Chirino observed that de Leon encouraged flagellation to be performed in tandem with the reading of the Miserere, a musical setting of the fifty-first Psalm, which emphasized the sinner's seeking of God's forgiveness. This tandem of flagellation and the mindfulness of atonement was a "holy exercise [that was] a source of great edifice to the Indians, and, in imitation of it, a great number of them took the discipline on those nights, in turn with the Spaniards (Chirino, quoted in Blair and Robertson 1903, 12:249).

There are indications of the continued conjunction of flagellation and the mindset of atonement, particularly in following the example of the exemplary figures of the Church, among "a great concourse of people" from the account of another Jesuit, Francisco Vaez, in 1601. Vaez reported, "The practice of 'scourging,' not as hitherto on three days in Lent, but every Friday throughout the year, in our Church. . . . On feast days, they spend the afternoons in listening to spiritual reading an in commemorating the examples of the saints" (F. Vaez, S.J. [1601] in Blair and Robertson 1903, 11:196–197).

Chirino continued to report that the dual technologies of self-flagellation and mindfulness of sin had been taken to with "extraordinary" vehemence by Filipino Christian converts (Chirino 1969, 285; Barker 1999, 6–7). In his 1604 *Relacion*, Chirino described how Filipinos of all walks of life remained "so eager and fervent" in the practice of flagellation that it was sometimes necessary to physically restrain determined converts from inflicting too much pain on their bodies. This finds corroboration in the account of another Jesuit, Gregorio Lopez, who recorded in 1605/1606 that the desire for atonement with God was far greater than the fear of physical pain endured in self-flagellation: "There was such readiness and pious anger against self that one person was forbidden to treat himself so severely. He asked: 'What is better, to save me with blood or suffer punishment of sin? When another was reprehended for living too free a life, he replied: 'You are right, father, I will avenge my sin; give me the scourge; the body is wild, it must be tamed.' He went into the church scourged himself until he judged he had punished himself sufficiently" (G. Lopez 1605, 276, quoted in Brewer 2004, 72).

Other religious orders recorded the same confluence between self-flagellation and desire for divine atonement. Given Saint Francis' own renowned enthusiasm for self-mortification, like the Jesuits, early Franciscan missionaries successfully inculcated the adoption of these twin technologies of flagellation and atonement in their evangelical regimen. In the Philippines, the Franciscans occupied the province of Camarines, composed of approximately 120 lay priests, preachers, and confessors as well as lay brothers (Schumacher 1979, 18). Franciscan Marcelo de Ribadeneira in 1601 spoke of "houses of persons of advanced virtue" in which acts of self-mortification, including flagellation, were conducted "many times to blood" with the official sanction of clerical authority. In fact, the vehemence with which these rituals were conducted sometimes required the regulation of the priests. Ribadeneira's observations are worth considering in full:

> It is quite ordinary for them to wear a sackcloth which is so rough that it is necessary to restrain them in this matter and in the continual bloody disciplines which they take, so that they may not destroy their natural strength. They likewise try to get up to pray in their houses when they hear the religious singing of the Matins, and at that time they commend themselves to God and give themselves to mental

prayer. From this practice many of these souls are advancing in spiritual progress.

When the time of Lent comes there are a few days in which the discipline is taken, and many times to blood. And they carry heavy crosses and perform other mortifications. . . . There are houses of persons of advanced virtue which are sort of hospices where the faithful join them to treat of God our Lord and to exercise themselves in penance and mortification. They ask each other to mortify them and to give them cause for merit, so that these houses are as it were places for spiritual souls. For in them they scourge themselves and ask that others scourge them. And some have themselves hang on a cross, others put great weights on their necks, others drag weights from a halter as if they were beasts, since they consider themselves such for having offended God. Others . . . keep their arms extended in the form of a cross for such a long time to cause wonder. The sightings and groanings with which they do all these things are many and deep, lamenting that they have offended the Divine Majesty. . . . Whoever should enter into the towns of these faithful in the time of Lent and in particular during all of Holy Week, would think rather that he is entering a monastery of religious of great penance rather than into towns or houses of ordinary lay people. (Ribadeneira, quoted in Schumacher 1979, 84–85; Ribadeneira [1601] 1947, 61, 62–63)

Ribadeneira provides a sense of the diversity of mortification practices in "ordinary lay people's" houses that effectively transform during Holy Week into centers of high piety. What is interesting and significant is that "spiritual advancement" is premised not upon the mere performance of various modes of physical self-mortification but on the act of "lamenting that they have offended the Divine Majesty" such that these places are transformed from "ordinary" houses to places of "great penance."

Other religious orders had a similarly high regard for mortification practices. Dominican Blancas de San Jose wrote poems in Tagalog to be read by converts in the 1640s. San Jose recommended self-inflicted pain as a means toward the attainment of transcendence when he wrote in Tagalog in 1645,

Woe to you, Christians.
Discipline your body
And regardless of what may happen
Strive to attain
And endeavor to find [salvation]. (Rafael 1988, 184)

There is also some archival evidence to suggest that rituals of self-mortification remained part of the colonial sensibility well into the eighteenth century. In his Kapampangan vocabulary list published in 1732, for example, Augustinian Fray Diego Bergaño defined "Disciplinarse" in terms of *"batbat,"* referring to "the whip, the lash. Matbabt, batbatan, to whip or beat. . . . The whipped or heated without being bound to something" (Bergaño [1732] 2007). This was a form of pious subjectivity based on the idea that there is a correlation between physical pain, moral responsibility, and pious subjective formation.

The Historicity of Suffering

In confronting the empirical conundrum that one encounters in asking about the origins of Passion rituals, the focus in this chapter has been on cultivating an attentiveness to both the continuities and discontinuities in the legacy of European ideas and practices in the Philippines. Europe, as the historian Dipesh Chakrabarty (2000, 16) observes, "is at once both indispensable and inadequate" in helping us think through the traces of colonial regimes, including that of contemporary religious life in Pampanga. Filipino practitioners of Passion rituals today may not consider their acts as an articulation of a specifically European or even foreign inheritance. Nevertheless, with a more nuanced reflection on the experience of Lito as representative of the ethnographic landscape in Pampanga, we find that Passion rituals in the Philippines are premised on a particular ideology that gained currency in a broader European discursive and historical milieu: that the suffering body is what God would consider "something good."

The first part of this chapter shed some light on the ideological conditions that established the normativity of "suffering," which revered individuals in the history of Christianity embodied as an equivalency between self-inflicted pain and religious piety. Like the early martyrs and the exemplary saints that followed them, early Christian monastics, and later the laity, subjected themselves to forms of bodily circumscription. Christian modes of *disciplina* were aimed at nothing less than a self-mastery of all aspects of one's being, including intellect, imagination, sensibility, and will. To mortify the flesh was to embody a pedagogy of self-denial that was based on the ideology that bodily pain had moral and an existential value.

It is with this ideological context that I considered, in the second part of this chapter, the archival sources that indicate the vehement introduction and encouragement of Passion rituals in the early part of the Spanish colonial regime. The accounts of missionaries from different religious orders is not just significant because they attest to the existence of self-flagellation in the early history of the Philippines. Missionary accounts consistently demonstrate how the inculcation of the discipline was strongly conditioned by the ideal tandem of atonement and self-flagellation. To be a disciplined convert was to be a self-policing colonial subject conditioned in mind, body, and spirit to believe in the equivalency between physical suffering through pain, mindfulness of sin, and the prospect of eventual spiritual deliverance.

It is important to note that the public performance of self-flagellation and other forms of mortification was affected by the official denunciation of flagellant processions that came along with the Spanish Bourbon reforms in the later half of the eighteenth century. These reforms instituted Enlightenment ideals that sought to improve the economic and political infrastructure of Spain and its colonies.[8] In 1777, Carlos III issued a royal decree that prohibited flagellation processions because instead of evoking its ostensible objectives of spiritual edification and repentance, it evoked "scorn from the prudent, amusement and uproar from the boys, and amazement, confusion and fear from children and women, and even more injurious results, rather than good example, or the expiation of sins" (Barker 1998, 3; Wroth 1991, 18).[9] Following suit, the Provincial Council in Manila was explicit in its declaration that "nobody should flog himself publicly in the streets or in churches during Holy week" (Barker 1998, 7, quoted in Barrion 1960, 304, 307).

In contrast to the enthusiastic declarations of its practice in the late sixteenth and early seventeenth centuries, there is relatively less mention in the historical archive of self-mortification being a formally sustained practice among the religious orders throughout the colonial regime in the Philippines. But rather than conclude that this was indicative of a decline in Filipino enthusiasm for the practice, it is more plausible that, as Nicholas Barker (1998, 7) argues, "the absence of references to flagellation was a deliberate act of self-censorship by the friars, not an indication of indigenous disinterest or disavowal. Among Filipinos, ritual self-flagellation continued unabated especially in the emerging epicenter of central Luzon."

Although official prohibitions against the practice may have eventually relegated flagellation to the private sphere, the most prominent historians of the Philippine colonial period (including, for example, Reynaldo Ileto and Vicente Rafael) have argued that Spanish missionaries continued to control the discourse and ideology of suffering through alternative means, specifically through modes of vernacular literature. As I show in the next chapter, religious texts such as the *pasyon* manifest the legacy of Spanish colonial attempts to transplant the normativity of suffering selfhood that they themselves inherited. The way Passion texts were thought of as a way to orient inner subjectivity toward suffering and atonement formed the basis for the continued perpetuation of forms of disciplina. In examining the continuing legacy of the pasyon—a fact mentioned by Lito and other self-flagellants—we can reconcile the archival footprint of disciplina with the way flagellants today understand and describe their ritual agency.

PART II

Investments

The Ensounded Body
The Aural Environment of Passion Chanting

Upon venturing into the town of San Pedro Cutud during Holy Week, the first thing that confronted me was the amplified voice of an elderly lady, who was making the most hauntingly lugubrious sound. It was the voice of Aling Cel, a fifty-year-old owner-operator of a small provision store in the town of San Fernando. Her voice spilled onto the streets through worn-down karaoke speakers, seemingly set to full blast. I was told by one of the bystanders that Aling Cel's morose vocalizing had been going on nonstop, all day and all night, for several days, drowning out even the sounds of passing tricycles, barking dogs, and the residual noise from people's TVs and karaoke sessions. These other sounds were discernible only in the gaps created by the frequent glitches in the grainy sound system. Amid the cacophony, there was something entrancing, even soothing, about Aling Cel's voice, which to me sounded like she was chanting a very sad song. It was not easy to decipher every word of the chant's "lyrics," which were expressed in the local dialect, Kapampangan. But one got the sense from the somber tone and long, melodramatic enunciation that Aling Cel was lamenting the loss of something, or someone, much loved and greatly revered. "It sounds like a wake," I said to my companion. "Well, I suppose it is . . . sort of," came his somewhat tentative reply.

What I describe is the *pabasa*: the public chanting of the narrative of the Passion of Christ, as it is read from a vernacular text called the *pasyon* during Holy Week.[1] The pabasa is a communal gathering typically organized by prominent families in a local town chapel or, if large enough, in a sponsor's home. The gathering features a number of chanters, gathering in groups of around a dozen, taking turns performing in a choral style called *lamentasyon* (lamentation). Makeniman, a companion of mine whose family has lived in Pampanga for generations, told me that the sound of the lamentasyon is the most distinctive aspect of cultural and religious life in Pampanga during this time. He describes it in one of his widely read online blog entries as a manifestation of the province's religious and cultural heritage: "The ritual acapella singing of the pasyon appears to mimic the pattern of church singing, [but] with deep influences from local folk melodies. The style is called miasmatic, characterized by highly florid passages in which the original tune is spun out into embellishments. The [pabasa] may vary from the very plaintive (*"managulele"*), mournful (*"dalit"*) to dirge-like (*"punebri"*)" (Castro 2007b).

To confront the pabasa as an experience of aurality is a major feature of a deeply sentimental experience of Holy week, one that is thick, saturated, with sound. Given its consuming acoustic texture, one might think of the encounter with the pabasa as an example of what composer R. Murray Schafer (1993, 91) described as *schizophonia*: a "synthetic soundscape in which natural sounds are becoming increasingly unnatural while machine-made substitutes are providing the operative signals directing modern life." This is a popular view conveyed by journalist Felice Santa Maria in a 1989 article titled "Passion Power." She writes, "Pasyon chanting is music to or murder on the ears depending not so much on the quality of the singing but the point of view adapted to the tradition" (Santa Maria 1989, 97). Taking exception to this depiction, Makeniman encouraged "a more nuanced ear" in telling me that Passion rituals cannot simply be described in terms of unnatural noise pollution. He would, I think, agree with the anthropologist Steven Feld (1996, 134), who observed, "Places make sense in good part because of how they are made sensual and how they are sensually "voiced." In this context, the scene we encounter in Holy Week "makes sense" if we look beyond the limitations imposed by our expectations about what is "noisy" and what is "musical" or "harmonious." Taking up Makeniman's prompting, then, I do not simply think of the pabasa experience as an acoustic residue of ritual action (what Santa Maria described as "murder on the ears") but as an aural sensorium—a dynamic of vocal projection and sonic immersion that cultivates modes of religious piety in and through the body's capacity to vocalize particular sentiments and emotions, along with the corresponding capacity to "hear" sounds in a particular way.

Social scientists working on sound, particularly those inspired by phenomenology, have analyzed the body and its senses as conduits toward a subject's accessing, perceiving, and being in the world (Jackson 1989; Stoller 1989; Porath 2008).[2] Along these lines, I propose to "hear" the pabasa as an "aural representation of culture" (Samuels et al. 2010, 335), one that can be grasped, as Feld recommends, by "confronting the intersection of musical, verbal, folkloric, literary, psychological, gender-related, and sociological constructs" (Feld 1990, 263). As such, I pursue in this chapter a convergence between, on the one hand, an anthropology of sensation that fosters a "sounded anthropology," and, on the other, a sociology of emotions, which posits how cohesive ritual interactions are cultivated in the sharing of emotional energy. I conduct this disciplinary convergence by tackling three distinct but interrelated topics.

First, I trace the pabasa in the legacy of how Spanish missionization sought to control and institutionalize the discourse and ideology of suffering selfhood through modes of vernacular devotional literature called the "pasyon." Examining the pasyon is particularly relevant in situating the normativity of "suffering selfhood" in its local Filipino context. But even more than that, the point of this section is to inquire into how the pious subjectivities that are crafted in the physical engagement with pasyon text—chanting or reading it in public, which is the family tradition alluded to by Lito Santos in the previous chapter—can be directly associated with the ritual agency that motivates and underscores the performance of Passion rituals in Pampanga, and perhaps beyond.

It is upon the backdrop of this history that I consider how the bodies of pabasa chanters like Aling Cel and her family become *ensounded*. The main observation I make here is that pious agency does not exclusively (or even primarily) result from acts of biblical exegesis but is, like Makeniman suggested, responsive to sonically projected deployments of emotions. That is to say that a chanter's religious subjectivity inheres in the state of being immersed in the pabasa's acoustic sensorium, itself made more meaningful in the chanter's efforts to "suffer through" the strain of vocalizing the emotional force of vernacular religious traditions like the pasyon.

Second, I shift the focus toward the "listeners" who are within the audible range of pabasa, who become, with the chanter, "fellow mourners" mutually implicated in the emotions of bereavement that are projected by the chanter's voice. It is in this context that I describe how the chanter's pious inner states—what in the vernacular is known as *lub*—are not private and "buffered" but are shared with others through the sonic projection of the amplified voice. This is tantamount to what sociologists such as Randall Collins have thought of as a form of emotional contagion, in which shared or outwardly projected emotions amplify visceral energies that enhance group solidarity and togetherness. In this way emotions are "contagious."

The contagion of pabasa sounds is the context for a discussion of how embodied Passion rituals such as self-flagellation occur within the aural sensorium that pabasa chanting cultivates. Third, I argue that a mode of emotional contagion occurs when rituals such as the pabasa and self-mortification reciprocally feed off each other, both drawing from the sonic energy modulated by the voice of chanters such as Aling Cel. This is not to say that emotional contagion is the only prerequisite for ritual agency. It is important to show, however, that sound exerts an attractive force that influences the pious itineraries and pathways of those corporeal rituals that give Holy Week in Pampanga such a distinctive character. More than just words read out loud, I would argue that the pabasa is primarily a visceral form of devoutness, one that commemorates Christ's martyric episode through the body's projection of and saturation in an aural sensorium.

To be sure, thinking about the pasyon and pabasa in this sensual-centric way is not intuitive to our scholarly understanding of Filipino vernacular religious traditions, which has been oriented primarily toward an interpretation of the meanings of texts and words. Historian Reynaldo Ileto's *Pasyon and Revolution: Popular Movements in the Philippines, 1896–1910* (1979) was a watershed in our understanding of the pasyon and how, in the reading and chanting of its words, Filipinos were able to connect tropes of Christ's suffering with their own status as oppressed colonial subjects.[3] Reading the archives "from below," Ileto's main concern was "to bring to light the masses' own categories of meaning that shaped their perceptions of events and their participation in them" (8). This focus on "categories of meaning" resonates the influence of Derrida's *Of Grammatology* (1976), which endorsed a movement away from the phonocentric idealization of voice and sound in favor of a textual deconstruction of vernacular texts.

Influential as Ileto's largely textual-archival analysis is, the political theorist Benedict Anderson observed that "*Pasyon and Revolution* has the grand diachronic range that is the province of the historian, but it does not, and cannot have the synchronic depth of a first-class anthropological work" (quoted in Love 2004, xii). In the same vein, historian Joseph Scalice (2009, 2) has argued that the pasyon must be "read with an attention to the significance derived from its performance, [so that] we arrive at a very different understanding of lower class consciousness than that which Ileto found." It is with this "sounding out" of the pabasa's embodied and sensual forms, a challenge to the epistemic primacy of "ocular-centric" historical approaches, that this chapter is concerned. The starting point for this discussion is that the ritual efficacy of the pabasa is predicated not on a person's ability to reflect upon or even decipher the text of the pasyon but on something more embodied, emotional, and visceral.

Pasyon and the Cultivation of Passion

Spanish clerics channeled the ideology of suffering selfhood by working with Filipino religious elites in placing greater emphasis on the translation and proliferation of biblically derived devotional literature. One such text, called the pasyon, was intended to extoll the positive valence of suffering through the sharing and retelling of Christ's Passion. Its structure is the quintilla of five lines of eight verses interspersed with didactic passages called *aral* (literally, "lessons"), which encourage reflection on each event of the pasyon story. The pasyon was meant not simply as a text to be read but as a text to be chanted and sung out loud in groups. In its vocalized form, the pasyon evoked the indigenous tradition of *dalit*, a pre-Hispanic oral poetic rendition that consists of four lines with eight syllables each. For the dalit, as cleric Gaspar de San Agustin described it, was "more grave and somber in a manner that Greeks and Latins called epic-dithyrambs" (Lumbera 1986, 32). In this sense, the dalit's tenor was considered particularly suited to the Spanish missionary agenda because it offered the appropriate motif for channeling the pathos of the Christian episode.

In Luzon, pasyon texts such as Gaspar Aquino de Belen's Tagalog version (1704) were widely circulated from the late seventeenth century onward. Unlike self-flagellation rituals, pasyons such as this were endorsed by the archbishop of Manila, who granted indulgence to those who read and chanted it. Several other versions were produced in the eighteenth century, including the Bisaya versions in 1738 and 1740 by Augustinian Juan Sanchez, and a Tagalog version in 1740 by Don Luis Guian (Irving 2010). By 1800, Augustinian Joachin Martinez de Zuñiga observed that the pasyon was not merely read in private as text but physically channeled through verse and chant in a multitude of contexts: "Both men and women are much attracted to reading verses. . . . Every night during Lent passing through the streets one can be sure to hear the Pasion de Nuestro Señor Jesucristo recited in verse in many houses" (quoted in Schumacher 1979, 179; see also Blanco 2009, 106). By the turn of the nineteenth century, the pasyon was considered "the social epic of the . . . Tagalogs and probably other lowland groups as well" (Ileto 1979, 14). An account from the early 1900s similarly testifies to the pasyon's widespread penetration, stating, "Everyone is obliged to read Jesus' book about his life. People sing every phrase about his life. You can hardly find a boy or girl, man or woman, who does not know how to sing those phrases from Jesus book" (Ileto 1979, 25; see also Penson 1917, 147).

Ileto's *Pasyon and Revolution* (1979) furnishes us with a fascinating insight into the historical precedence for this process. In reading and chanting the pasyon, Ileto argues, Filipinos connected the meanings of Christ's suffering with their own status as oppressed colonial subjects, orienting themselves toward a new kind of collective soteriology premised on the deferred rewards of martyric suffering. In this sense, the Filipino engagement with the pasyon brings to mind how the ideology of suffering selfhood was cultivated by the early followers of Christianity. Punishment, hardship, and pain—vicissitudes that were part of the experience of early Christian martyrs as well as colonial subjects—were seen not as manifestations of hopeless oppression but as facilitators toward the purification of interior states so that the pious could eventually arrive at ultimate and "victorious" salvation.

The most common pasyon chanted in Pampanga, and the one still widely used today, is the version attributed to native secular priest Dr. Mariano Pilapil. Written in 1814, it is known as the "Pasiung Henesis," or the "Pasiung Pilapil."[4] It is this pasyon that flagellants in Pampanga refer to as central to their original motivations for ritual practice, particularly when passages from these versions are sung or chanted with expressions of grief, tearful weeping, and sometimes wailing. Indeed, the text itself is replete with themes of sorrow and compassion, evoking sentiments that are commensurate in spirit with the motivations for self-flagellation.

But more than this emotional contagion between chanting and flagellating, the pasyon is resonant because it emphasized, in the words of one fla-gellant, Lito Santos, the inner heaviness (*bigat ng loob*) as a basis for chan-neling a solidarity with Christ's own suffering. The pasyon, in this sense, remains widely acknowledged as a basis for the physical enactment of Passion rituals because it presented a backdrop for a deeply sentimental identification with Christ's own act of self-sacrifice. We now turn to how the pabasa is embodied.

The Passion Chanter's Ensounded Body

In this section, I discuss how the meaningfulness of the pabasa is contin-gent upon a how a chanter can become "ensounded." In examining this, it is important to focus beyond the act of vocalizing sounds, including the corporeal context in which those vocalizations are made. Just as import-ant as the sound is how the chanter's body confronts the arising chal-lenges of distraction, tolerance, or fatigue. For the act of chanting itself tests the body's tolerances and capacities, such that persevering is itself a form of pious discipline. I return to the ethnographic incident I described earlier in this chapter in order to delve into the sensory experience of the pabasa—both for the chanter and for those who are caught up in its audible range.

As I drew closer to the source of the chanting in San Fernando, I observed a few people gathered outside a *puni*—a small, makeshift building made out of plywood that functions as a temporary minichapel for housing pasyon chanters.[5] A sign outside the structure—each letter painted on cir-cular containers typically used to carry uncooked rice—read "Pabasa 2010" (literally, "Reading 2010"). Close physical proximity to the pabasa allows one to appreciate the observations of historical musicologist D. R. M. Irving (2010, 151), who describes the Passion rituals in the Philippines as "a per-formative foundation for devotions to the Passion of Christ, in terms of mourning for and extolling a great deceased hero."

I glanced inside and saw the focal point of the vocally "mourning" crowd: a small table covered with a white cloth and adorned with flowers and candles. There was a crucifix, as well as a statue of a patron saint po-sitioned at the center of the table. It looked like any altar one might see in a chapel, except for the absence of some vital components, namely the Eucharist, the Bible, and an officiating priest.[6] There was an old dilapi-dated book from which the chanters would melodically "read" out loud the Passion of Christ. Their words—flowing and morose—were enunci-ated through two microphones connected to old box-type speakers hidden behind the centerpiece table.

Although the auditory environment that dominates this scenario is typ-ically sustained by a single chanting voice, it is common for a chanter to hand over the chanting duties to a companion. Indeed, the format of the pabasa lends itself to this kind of interactivity. The chanter reads out the pabasa in five-line stanzas in the poetic form of the Spanish quintillo. In this form, each line has eight syllables, and, according to ethnomusicologist Ric Trimillos (1992, 7), typically has "forty text events per stanza." The vocalization can be described as antiphonal, whereby a chanter performed a certain number of stanzas in resounding and evocative tone before handing over to another chanter waiting nearby.

After about half an hour of chanting, Aling Cel passed the microphone to a younger lady, her teenaged daughter Rowena, who then took over the chanting from where her mother left off. That would have been Rowena's fourth "shift." While there did not seem to be any rules stipulating how long a person was meant to chant, I was told that it was unusual for anyone to take a shift of anything less than a three to four hours.[7] The younger chanter seemed to take some liberty with the chanting, adding to it a kind of flourish that made for a distinct departure in style and form.

The words of the chanted pasyon text are not made clearer or more comprehensible by the microphones. Actually, the opposite is true, since in most cases the microphones produce a grainy or muffled acoustic texture that often renders many of the chanted words indecipherable, even to those proficient in the vernacular. The effect of electric amplification is that it produces variations in the cadence and harmonization of chanting—some louder and more modulated, others more a monotone droll, some male, others female—resulting in inconsistent pieces and pitches of acoustic projection. In many cases, the microphone would go off intermittently, if not completely, making it unlikely that one would be able to take in the whole of the pabasa's message. In any case, unless one sits through the pabasa for its duration (that is, for several days and nights leading up to Good Friday), it is only ever possible to piece together meaningful snippets of decipherable words.

The efficacy of the pabasa, however, is not contingent upon a general cognition of the precise details of the pasyon text. Indeed, its visceral impact is independent of the referential function of language to express sentiments of grief and mourning. The vocalization of deeply held sentiments renders the body ensounded, as Tim Ingold describes it (2011, 139). Like the ritual wailing described by the anthropologist Greg Urban (1988, 398), the pabasa "[does] not require that the beacon of consciousness be cast upon the underlying signaling phenomenon. The signaling phenomenon itself occurs at a less than fully conscious plane." Given its limited comprehensibility, what is dominant in the experience of the pabasa is the aural ambiance that is produced by the chanter's voices, which, while inconsistent, nevertheless cultivate a somber, melodramatic experience. In this sense, the pabasa inculcates not deciphering per se but aural metasignals of bereavement that evoke a commiseration with the chanter's grief.

After a significant amount of time chanting, I observed that Rowena began to slouch awkwardly, barely able to keep the microphone up to her mouth as she fanned herself profusely with her other hand. Rowena's voice seemed tired and hoarse. I noticed the same effect among other pabasa chanters, particularly during the later hours and the early morning. The discomfort of vocalizing for long hours, often in the same seated position, would put a physical strain on the body that became obvious in the affecting of the tone and intensity of the chant. Aside from this, pabasa chanting would take a mental strain as well. On two or three different occasions, I observed chanters who would fidget with their cellphones even while maintaining the chant.

If one were to take this aspect of the pabasa at face value, it might be said that the pabasa classifies as a failed ritual according to conventional analyses of ritual, particularly in the microsociological tradition inspired by Émile Durkheim and Erving Goffman. The sociologist Randall Collins, in his book *Interaction Ritual Chains* (2004, 51), described the main feature of a failed ritual as possessing "a sense of a drag, the feeling of boredom and constraint, even depression, interaction fatigue, a desire to escape."[8] Collins concedes that even a failed ritual may succeed—that is to say, it amplifies emotional energy in a way that enhances reverence for sacred objects and symbols—when ritual actors such as Rowena become "entrained into showing [a] greater level of animated involvement" (53). However, Collins states, this "forced" level of involvement is not intrinsic to the "natural" energy inherent in ritual action: "they feel forced insofar as the level of collective effervescence is higher than it would be normally given the existing ingredients of shared attention and emotional stimulus; the mutual entrainment has an element of deliberation and self-consciousness rather than a natural flow" (53).

I had a chance to ask Rowena about the uncomfortable and distracting aspect of the pabasa later, and whether participating in pabasa is forced (*napipilitan*). Rowena told me that the discomfort and fatigue are only "natural" during pabasa chanting. Rather than feeling forced, Rowena chose to persevere through the hardship of chanting—inflicting upon herself a kind of bodily circumscription, one that is commensurate with the "natural flow" of commemorating Christ's sacrifice. "This is Holy Week. We're supposed to make sacrifices," she underscored. While it is true that some chanters make an effort to imbue the pabasa with a certain performative aesthetic, one that emphasizes the skillfulness of the chanters delivery, the "success" or "failure" of the chant is not measured primarily by acoustic virtuosity. Rather, it is precisely the hoarseness of the chanter's voice that is seen as indicative of the extent of her pious commitment to particular religious expectations. For the chanter, the pabasa is not a passive act of reading alone but also an opportunity to embody a sacrifice that approximates that of Christ's own.

To chant was to project not words and meanings but tones and reverberations that, in the wariness, strain, and fatigue of the voice, resonated an identification with the pathos of Christ's sacrificial ordeal. Chanting in this sense is a challenging mode of self-discipline tantamount to a voluntary infliction of strain and discomfort upon the body. For to chant in this way is to reference Christ's own tumultuous ordeal. Chanting is, in that sense, a form of sonic piety whereby disciplined ritual action is premised upon the visceral production of aurality.

This sonic energy that emanates from the chanters conditions a sensorium of empathic mourning, one that invites anyone, regardless of their relationship to the "deceased," to share in a common intersubjective space. Listening to the chant, even from afar, one cannot help but feel implicated in aurally carried emotional energy—as though you, too, have lost a loved one, and that those within earshot are bound to you in a collective experience of bereavement. We now turn to the morose sociality of the pabasa.

Fellow Mourners in Sound

Thus far I have discussed how pabasa is meaningful in channeling the ritual agency of individual chanters. In this section, the focus is on how pabasa is also a communal activity in which ritual participants inhabit a sonically amplified aural space of shared emotion. Passion rituals can be seen, as the anthropologist Fenella Cannell (1995, 383) has observed, as "a scene which in several ways resembles the co-operative neighborliness of a wake." The aural environment conditioned by the sounds of pabasa evoke an entire ensemble of cultural and religious referents—especially relating to empathy and bereavement—such that the pabasa is not just a vocalization of text but an audible projection of sorrow as well. As such, even those who are not chanting become "contaminated" with emotions of grief and mourning, projected outward through the vibrations and resonations of the chanter's voice.

In Aling Cel's pabasa, visitors from all walks of life—relatives, friends, and not a few prominent members of local government—came to spend some time in the puni. Everyone gathered at Aling Cel's house was effectively enjoined to partake in a collective reliving every second of the physical suffering that preceded Christ's death.[9] All the guests were attended to by Jem, Aling Cel's son, who brought out a small plastic stool for each visitor to sit on. Visitors were not expected to chant along verbatim— indeed, they had no immediate access to the text from which the chanters read. Nevertheless, whoever enters effectively contributes to the somber atmosphere of collective mourning, even by just sitting in silence or, as I observed at times of those present, by vocalizing an audible moan of grief from time to time.[10] Sensing that I had come with a companion who was somewhat hesitant to intrude, Aling Cel reiterated this by moving her hands in a gesture of invitation: "Come and join," she said to my companion. "We are not acquainted, but you are fellow mourners also . . . you are extending your inner self in good faith to others [*nag mamagandang loob sa kapwa*] in coming here, so of course I want you to feel welcome." It is significant that Aling Cel described visitors to the pabasa as "fellow mourners" who may not have a previous relationship with the host but have made a conscious decision to enter into the aural space of piety, thereby extending their "inner self in good faith to others" (nag mamagandang loob sa kapwa).

During a break from her "shift," Aling Cel came up to where I was sitting and offered me a plastic cup of mineral water, nodding her head in appreciation of my presence. Whispering through the chanting, I asked her what the pabasa meant to her. One of the first things she mentioned was that it was not so much a deep reflection on the specific meaning of the words that she chants. "Just with my voice, I already feel like I'm expressing empathy [*pakikiramay*] with [Jesus]," she said. "It's like making sounds of mourning is a way to remember his sacrifice." The word Aling Cel used to describe the experience, *pakikiramay*, means "to express sympathy," specifically in the context of the sorrow felt for the loss of a loved one. In the act of pakikiramay, the frame of reference for sympathy is based on imagining how the self would feel/respond if placed in a similar predicament. This personal frame of reference becomes the basis for commiserating or "feeling sorry" (*awa*) for the other person's suffering. In this context, sympathy is not just a cognitive capacity but also an "emotional reactivity in encountering another person, particularly when perceiving another person's suffering or distress" (Stueber 2010).

In the pabasa, however, chanters and overhearers alike are not "sad" in the conventional sense that one might expect at a wake. It is important to note that pakikiramay indexes not an individual's private, self-contained feelings of despair but the mode of consociation that is channeled when grief is shared in "culturally specific and performatively evocative ways" (Feld 1990, 264). Indeed, the meaningfulness of the pabasa is directly related to pakikiramay as a specific kind of intersubjectivity and fellow-beingness. As Aling Cel explains, "Firstly, we do this because it's our family tradition. But also we gather because we are like fellow mourners who remember what Christ went through."

On the surface, it might be said that to be "copresent" in the pabasa is to be exposed to an experience of emotional contagion in which there is an almost involuntary transfer of sorrowful emotions between inter subjects. From a neuropsychological standpoint, Elaine Hatfield, John T. Cacioppo, and Richard L. Rapson (1994, 5) define emotional contagion as "an attentional and behavioral synchrony" between two individuals that emerges from "the tendency to automatically mimic and synchronize facial expressions, vocalizations, postures, and movements with those of another person's." Significantly, the research suggests that emotional contagion "has the same adaptive utility (and drawbacks) for social entities (dyads, groups) as [it] has emotion for the individual" (153). That emotional contagion occurs and has a large impact on the bonds people share with one another resonates with sociologists of emotions, and even among the pioneers of the sociological discipline itself, such as Émile Durkheim, who has famously agued in *The Elementary Forms of Religious Life* (1912) that collective rituals engender collectively effervescent modes of emotional entrainment. Following from Durkheim, Randall Collins has argued that long-term feelings of solidarity and group attachment are produced as the outcome of "a successful buildup of emotional coordination within an interaction ritual" (R. Collins 2004, 108). In the pabasa, sorrowful emotions that are shared in pakikiramay are amplified as aural metasignals through vocal projections, thus producing modes of social solidarity and fellow-beingness.[11]

Indeed, it is not hard to feel "contaminated" by collective emotions of sorrow when one is among pabasa chanters in the puni. To be sure, those immediately copresent are not necessarily expected to learn or memorize specific words verbatim in order to participate.[12] Aling Cel described those who "overhear" the pabasa as people who "catch" or are "contaminated" (*nahawa*) by the chanter's inner self—his or her *lub*. Conventionally defined, *lub* means "that which is inside," and as such refers to pure inner states that are subject to personal cultivation and nourishment. In this sense, *lub* is understood as first-person ontology, denoting a sense of what philosopher Charles Taylor (2008) would refer to as a "buffered selfhood" with "a much firmer sense of the boundary between self and other." Aling Cel's idea of lub resonates with that of anthropologist Albert Alejo, who recognizes how lub is a concept that is by its nature outwardly relational: "Our terms of sociability implies lub. . . . In essence, lub is a concept that has to do with relationality. This is not just a measure of subjectivity as selfhood, but a measure of subjectivity as part of others" (Alejo 1990, 30, translated from Tagalog). The lub that is channeled in pabasa chanting, however, is characterized by a kind of porosity of the self—which renders one's inner being to be susceptible to emotional contagion and group solidarity.

Significantly, Aling Cel describes the chanter's lub as oriented to and contaminated by "*kapwa.*" In the philosopher Katrin De Guia's (2008, 2) terms, kapwa is a "shared self" in which one "opens up the heart-doors of the 'I' to include the Other. . . . It thrives on basic connectedness—of man with man, of man with nature, of man with the unseen spirit worlds and, ultimately, of man with God." For psychologist Virgilio Enriquez, kapwa manifests shared identity such that "the ako (ego) and the iba-sa-akin (others) are one and the same in kapwa psychology" (Gripaldo 2005, 10). Seen in terms of kapwa, the pabasa chant is not simply the expression of personal, individual loss but also a mode of implicating others in an emotionally contagious sorrow. The pabasa, then, is a vocal externalization of both ontological and intersubjective selfhoods.[13] In describing the pabasa in terms of kapwa, Aling Cel points to her chanting as an arena for the cultivation of mournful emotions that uses the text of the pasyon as a template for communal, intersubjective bereavement and group solidarity.

What I would like to turn to at this juncture is how this specific auditory environment is not just about cultivating interior states of piety but also about encouraging ritualized corporeal actions among those who "overhear" the pabasa. As I described at the beginning of this chapter, the pabasa is a visceral experience felt far beyond the immediate vicinity of its vocalization. The sonic reach of the pabasa—that is to say the range of its emotional contagiousness—cannot be neatly confined or emplaced in a single space. As a projection of lub with one's kapwa, the pabasa is effectively a broadcasted "meta-affect" that motivates others to engage in specific kinds of ritual actions. We shall now turn to the kinds of ritual expressions that are inspired by the pabasa's emotional contagion.

The Pabasa's Contagiousness

The previous two sections of this chapter have demonstrated that the sonic ambiance of pabasa chanting engenders a form of emotional contagion, one in which those within audible range become emotionally "contaminated" by the vocally projected sentiments of grief and bereavement. This contagion is not premised upon a perfect semantic cognition of text. As Reynaldo Ileto has observed, the engagement with the pabasa was "one of feelings, not of deciphering or understanding. What, to others, might have seemed like noise was, to the pilgrims, similar to music in a key that their religious experience enabled them to respond to" (Ileto 1979, 66). In this section I examine how this emotional contagion affects the ritual agencies outside of the immediate spatial domain of the chanting sessions. That is, to ask, how do the sounds of the pabasa serve as an aural signpost in which in the ritual itineraries of those performing Holy Week Passion rituals—particularly acts self-flagellation—become energized and embodied? Gaining insight on these matters would require focusing attention on what happens outside the puni.

While attending a pabasa in the days leading to Holy Week the year after my encounter with Aling Cel, I heard a distinct sound through the morose and somber tones of bereavement. The rhythm was a familiar one, several small, light sticks slapping repeatedly against a soft, moist surface of skin. Walking slowly in our direction was a man, hooded and blindfolded, swinging a whip around his bare back, which was bloodied from the repetitive self-flogging. Thick droplets flew off the cluster of wooden sticks at the end of his swaying rope. Stopping right outside the makeshift chapel, he continued flagellating in a kneeling position until finally he lay stomach-down on the ground, the flesh wound on his back shimmering in the blazing sun.

As if on cue, two men approached and took turns walloping the flagellant's buttocks and lower thighs—as hard as they were able, so it seemed—with wads of old newspapers rolled up into solid rods. The sound of the blows produced a kind of rhythm with the continuing chant, though it did not seem like this was intentional. The flagellant did not react, nor make any sound. In fact he appeared as though he were momentarily resting, his eyes remaining closed in spite of the firm whacks on his backside. His companions carried implements that belied a somewhat contradictory role in this scenario. Amid all of interaction between the flagellant and his companions, the cantillating chant of the pabasa continued uninterrupted, without so much as a pause. The gathered crowd seemed to share in the flagellant's pain, if only vicariously, with the occasional sigh and grimace and, once in a while, an exhale that seemed to signify an identification with the flagellant's ordeal. Before long, the beatings stopped, and the flagellant calmly picked himself up, resumed his whippings, and continued on his way.

Aling Cel told me that while they do not specifically chant to attract flagellants, they do not turn them away either: "They just turn up from time to time; they have their own vows to fulfill during Holy Week, we all do, so we don't mind sharing the space." Before the team of flagellants departed, I had a chance to speak to the young man accompanying the flagellant who is typically known as the latter's *sunod*, or, literally, his "follower." The sunod told me that it is not the chanted words per se that bring the flagellants to the puni but rather the sounds that emanate from them. "This is part of our ritual. We are guided by the sounds of the pabasa because it makes us feel like Holy Week is here," replied the sunod. "We don't have a [schedule] . . . we just allow the chants to guide our [flagellation] . . . it's more meaningful when you flagellate with the right 'soundtrack.' "

In the next few hours, flagellants and other Passion ritual practitioners would arrive in the puni. There were those who were performing the *mamusan Krus* (literally, carrying the cross), in which blindfolded men dressed in robes carried a heavy cross on their shoulder, dragging it around town for three to ten kilometers. Variations on this would have the cross tied with a rope to a person's back such that they would arch their back in order to lift the cross completely off the ground. Others perform a ritual called *pamagsalibatbat* in which hooded men or women crawl and squirm on the earthen ground toward a Church or puni. Pamagsalibatbat penitents sometimes conduct the ritual in pairs, tied together by a rope all throughout the journey along the ground. Like the flagellants, these devotees would be accompanied by one or two sunod, who act to guide their journey along the sounds of pabasa chanting.

The capacity of the pabasa to have this centripetal effect on the ritual agent's movement is to a great extent a function of technological mediations. Microphones have had the effect of projecting sentiments of affect of the chanter and yet in a way enables one to trace its origins, connecting those who hear it to the place whence it emanates (Samuels et al. 2010, 330). Murray Schafer's concept of soundscape laments synthetic sound as an artificial pollutant. Far from being a pollutant, the aural landscape of Holy

Week is characterized by the amplification of the emotional contagiousness of sounds produced from within the puni. Although placing primacy on rituals that have "full bodily assembly," the sociologist Randall Collins (2004, 60) acknowledged that "distance media," such as broadcasting over the airwaves or radio, can "provide some of the sense of shared attention and emotion, which gives a feeling of attraction, membership, and respect."

The immediate vicinity of the puni effectively become nodes at which two ways of commemorating Christ's Passion intersect—that of the flagellants, who embody Christ's somatic ordeal, and that of the chanter, who vocalizes a lamentation for His sacrificial act. In this way pabasa and Passion rituals exist in the same "sonorous enculturated world" (Samuels et al. 2010, 330), as ritual acts feeding into each other, "sharing the space" and together producing a common acoustic milieu. Stopping at this place, those performing Passion rituals are not so much worshipping in a liturgical sense, or even engaging in the act of listening. To stop at the puni is to soak up pious sonic energy, to saturate oneself with mournful vibes and reverberations, which are externalizations of those sentiments of bereavement that undergird the embodiment of Christ's pain. Rather than being attached to a particularly meaningful enunciation of words, their ritual itineraries are determined by the morose ambiance produced by the chanter's vocalization of the pasyon.

It might be said that the connection between pabasa and embodied Passion rituals such as flagellation manifests an "interactive ritual chain" (IRC). A theory developed by Randall Collins (2004) drawing inspiration from the work of Émile Durkheim ([1912] 2008) and Erving Goffman (1959; 1967), IRC asserts that ritual encounters are connected by chains of positive "emotional energy." The strength of these interactions depends on certain factors, including the physical, embodied "co-presence" of interactants, a common focus on a ritual object, a mutually shared "mood" of interaction, and synchronization of bodily movement and gesture. IRC theory is, therefore, one that posits a link between ritual agency, affect, and belief. As the sociologist Gary Alan Fine (2005, 1287) puts it, for Collins "affect is the engine of social order."

Collins (2004, 54) argues that "successful" rituals (that is to say, rituals that produce and amplify strong, positive emotional energies) can take place only where there is face-to-face interaction. In the mutual reading of and responding to facial gestures processes of "contagious emotional behaviors" can generate group solidarity and togetherness. Recognition of facial features, however, is not a significant factor in the convergence of pabasa and embodied Passion rituals such as flagellation, which are performed by people who are blindfolded or wear a cloth to cover their faces. Rather, it is the amplified sound of chanting that evokes the emotional and affective domains of human sensation. It is in this context that anthropologist Charles Hirschkind (2006, 79) speaks of the formation of a "pious sensorium" in which "listening invests the body with affective potentialities, depositing them in the pre-conscious folds of kinesthetic and synesthetic experience and, in doing so, endows it with the receptive capacities of the sensitive heart, the primary organ of moral knowledge and action."[14] Flagellants respond to the pabasa—sensually and logistically—because of the semantic openness of meta-affect, an effect of individual words congealing into one another to produce spaces of acoustic viscerality, projected out of the puni in sync with the sonic piety of pious bereavement.

The Aurality of Suffering

In channeling the disciplinary convergence between a "sounded" anthropology of sensation and a sociology of emotions and group dynamics, I have sought take heed of Makeniman's encouragement to go beyond musicality or textuality so that we might appreciate how chanted sounds evoke the wellspring of sensuous and religious sentiments that one encounters in Pampanga during Holy Week.

One of the more prominent ways scholars have described this aural scenario has been to evoke the concept of "soundscape," a term popularized by composer R. Murray Schafer, who, in his 1977 book *The Tuning of the World*, drew much-needed attention away from the visual toward the sensual realm of sound and how it constituted synthetic acoustic landscapes.[15] Yet to reduce the experience of pabasa to a "scape" of artificial sound would be tantamount to ignoring Makeniman's invitation for a "more nuanced ear" in understanding how the sound of devotional practices is crucial in shaping of pious personhoods, both for the chanter and for those ritual protagonists who are within the pabasa's audible range.

The concern of the first part of this chapter was to expand the empirical horizons of the historian Reynaldo Ileto's archival treatment of the pasyon in fostering what anthropologist David W. Samuels has called a "sounded anthropology"—one that attends to "sonorous enculturated worlds inhabited by people" (Samuels et al. 2010, 330). Commemorating Christ's Passion finds its most ideal expression when chanters "suffer" through physical and mental strain to produce vocally stylistic, melismatic outpourings of grief and bereavement. In so doing, ritual agents amplify and project their inner states—lub—thereby contaminating those within earshot with sorrowful emotions. Chanting projects a distinctive aural metasignal, one that saturates the landscape and effectively fosters a specific kind of emotional contagion.

In thinking about how the pabasa cultivates an intersubjective emotional contagion, we can understand why embodied Passion rituals are practiced in such great numbers in Pampanga province (as opposed to the entire Christianized Philippines). In elucidating how acoustic environments are constitutive of corporeal ritual acts, I have shown how religious agencies are responsive to specific tones, reverberations, and vibrations projected in and through the outward externalization of religious sensibilities.

Pagdarame

Self-Flagellation as Triangulated Empathy

When heading out to observe self-flagellation rituals in Pampanga, one must always carry an umbrella. That was the one piece of advice I had neglected to heed in my rush to set out for fieldwork on a sunny Good Friday morning in 2013. The moment I stepped out onto the street, there were already scores of shirtless, blindfolded, barefooted men conducting the famous rituals of self-flagellation—rituals that the anthropologist Fernando Zialcita (2000, 16) has described as "self-punishments [that] must be bloody." On that day there were perhaps a hundred men swinging whips around their upper torsos, aggravating freshly inflicted wounds on profusely bleeding flesh. Blood flowed down along their backs, coagulating and drying on stained-red trousers. Inevitably, thick red droplets of blood flung outward, propelled by the whip's swinging motion, prompting bystanders to protect themselves by unfurling their umbrellas horizontally in front of them. In the midst of this, I had veered too close and was sprayed by blood from one of the flagellant's whips. Seeing the resulting red blots on my clothes and skin, a young boy approached and cried out, almost laughing: "You have their blood on you, *kuya* [older brother]! Didn't you bring an umbrella?"

Rituals of self-flagellation have been so ingrained in the cultural experience of Holy Week in Pampanga that there are words that describe even its most minute aspects in Augustinian Friar Diego Bergaño's 1732 *Vocabulario de Pampango en Romance* (The vocabulary of the Kapampangan language). Given the scene I have just described, one might think that the most apt among these words is *talangdang*, which means "to be thrown off, like the drops of blood being deflected from the discipline of the penitents." However, self-flagellants themselves hardly use this word when asked to describe their ritual. Instead, the physical and emotional components of self-flagellating are popularly known as *pagdarame*, and practitioners of self-flagellation are called *magdarame*. Father Bergaño defines the root of "pagdarame," *dame*, as a "sharing or participating in a work." The prominent Kapampangan scholar Robert Tantingco (2006, 106) further elaborates in suggesting that "pagdarame" means "more or less the same as the Tagalog damay," which the historian Reynaldo Ileto (1979, 65) defined as "sympathy and/or condolence for another's misfortune".

The widespread use of "pagdarame" to describe self-flagellation encourages us to consider a counterintuitive notion about ritual agency in Pampanga: that in conducting these pious acts, ritual practitioners do not focus on the bloodiness of the ritual, but on modes of suffering external to themselves. This points to a mode of ritual agency that is premised upon a sense of mutual implication and empathic engagement in the predicament of others. Self-flagellation, in short, is not about how a painful and bloody experience can help one go to heaven. It is about relating to the predicament and suffering of one's coevals (Fabian 1983), and seeking, through one's body, to facilitate an improvement in another's well-being through ritual means.

Popular awareness about self-flagellation rituals is conditioned by depictions that hamper our ability to appreciate the complex dynamics of the local agencies that motivate them. Most of the works that have been written about them assume that the rationale of self-flagellation is a literalist appropriation of imported Spanish Catholic customs centered upon the achievement of atonement. However, the vast majority of ritual flagellants that I have spoken to in Pampanga have not described their ritual motivations in terms of sinfulness or the desire for divine reconciliation. This is an observation echoed by others who have studied the ritual, such as anthropologists Nicholas Barker (1998), Peter Bräunlein (2009, 2010a), and Fernando Zialcita (1986), as well as Alfredo Evangelista (1962, 11), who claimed that "not a single vow of the 30 cases [of self-flagellation] was a result of repentance or sin."

This misimpression of local ritual agency is compounded by the fact that the exact scale of pagdarame in Pampanga, let alone the Philippines, is not easy to establish. Barker (1998, 8) estimated that since the 1950s in Pampanga, "tens of thousands of Filipino men scourged themselves during Holy Week in a dramatic spectacle of public blood-letting." A survey of nearly ten thousand practicing Catholics conducted by Verbite cleric and scholar Benigno Beltran (1987, 62) in the 1980s found that "36.3 % of the men had at some point inflicted pain on themselves for religious reasons." In the nearby province of Bulacan, Peter Bräunlein (2009, 898) observed that in the 1990s, "hundreds of flagellants and other penitents can be seen in [the town of] Kapitangan, especially on Good Friday." Theatre studies scholar Sir Anril Tiatco (2016, 7), in the 2000s, provided a more conservative estimate in San Fernando City, where, he wrote, "about 100 [flagellants] are reported to participate." Provincial or municipal authorities in the province do not have a consistent method of official record keeping of the numbers of magdarame on any given year. When I spoke to him in 2010, a village headman of San Pedro Cutud in San Fernando estimated the number at "at least one thousand" but explained that it is precisely the sheer volume of magdarame that prevents any meaningful recording of statistics. "There [are] just too many people doing it," he said, exasperated, "it seems senseless to count." Marnie Castro, an official of the city government who is in charge of organizing Holy Week commemorations, estimated the number at "more than two thousand" (Sapnu 2013).

It is against this backdrop of such quantitative inconsistencies and knowledge deficits, compounded by the prevalent interest in the bloody and macabre aspects of the rituals, that I examine the contours of the religious agencies that are embodied in the performance of pagdarame. Just by actually witnessing the Holy Week scene in the province, it is not a far stretch to accept that the rituals are conducted by a great number of people. What is not immediately apparent is the intended result sought by ritual self-flagellants. What kind of emotional and sentimental meanings underscore these gruesome corporeal acts? How is the body-in-pain seen as a way to address these sentiments and intentions? The main point I make in response to these questions is that a person who self-flagellates "suffers" so that they can cultivate a particular kind of intersubjective personhood, one in which empathy between himself, God, and someone else who is held dear is paramount. It is only in the context of this kind of ritual agency, which I call triangulated empathy, that the desired outcome of pagdarame can be achieved—that is, an alleviation of the suffering of others, and an improvement in the life circumstances of those involved.

In the first part of this chapter, I describe the phenomenological experience of horizontal group dynamics in self-flagellation. Following that, I discuss how empathy has been conceptualized from a more conventional scientific and humanistic standpoint. I then present ethnographic portraits of how, when channeled into ritual domains, pagdarame demonstrates the limits of those conventional understandings. In so doing we can come to an appreciation of the sentimental and emotional underpinnings of tripartite empathic relations that motivate ritual action in Pampanga.

Limbon and Horizontal Sociality

Although rituals of pagdarame channel themes and an aesthetic that evoke the Passion story, they are not endorsed by the official Catholic Church in the Philippines. It is true, as I have argued, that these embodied acts can be traced to the legacy of Roman Catholicism. Nevertheless, the extreme severity and literalism of the rituals are officially discouraged by the Filipino religious hierarchy, many of whom disavow them as archaic and misguided ways of practicing the faith.

Far from a formal, sacramental rite, a group procession of magdarame—also known locally as a *limbon*—might easily be observed to be but a casual gathering of friends and acquaintances. For when magdarame converge, typically along sidewalks or alleyways near Pampanga's main arterial roads, it is not uncommon to find groups of as many as forty individuals happily consuming bottles of Red Horse beer and a few eggs, typically taken raw. To be sure, there are "serious" and specifically pious individual motivations that underlie the practice, which we shall discuss in more detail as this chapter unfolds. I evoke this scene because an understanding of these ritual motivations starts not with a strong aware-ness of the theology of imitating Christ but with an appreciation of the horizontal bonds of sociality and fellow feeling that enable and facilitate the ritual itself.

Even before individual acts of pagdarame begin in earnest, it is clear that the rituals are a multiperson affair. Each of the men in the limbon is accompanied by one or two companions, called *sunod* (literally, "to follow"). The sunod carry items that are interesting in their contrasting functions. One the one hand, they usually have bottles of water and a plastic water sprayer to soothe and relieve the flagellants along their journey. On the other, they also bear a set of implements and items of clothing designed for inflicting pain and preserving anonymity. These include a *burillo*, a custom-made whip made of rope with a set of five or six wooden sticks about two inches long attached to one end; a *binidbid*, a rope tied around the flagellant's torso and limbs; a crown made of dethorned vines, leaves, and twigs; and a stack of newspapers rolled into a firm baton.

The sunod play a crucial role in facilitating the blood letting that is fundamental in the act of self-flagellation itself. The flagellants would first slap their backs with the burillo with just enough force to stimulate the blood vessels, causing their backs to flush red and swell. They would then submit themselves to their sunod, who would each use a small knife called a *panabad* to make up to twenty-five small but fairly deep incisions (the *abad*) on the flesh of the back. Over the years, I was told, men in Pampanga had learned to make this process more efficient by us-ing an implement containing "nine sharpened pieces of glass from Coke bottles, embedded in solidified resin in a solid wooden handle shaped a paddle" (Barker 1998, 26). Instead of making single incisions with the panabad, the sunod—at this time taking the role of a *berdugo* (literally, "executioner")—would simply "dab" the flagellant's flesh four times. The resulting cuts would produce small droplets of blood that trickled down the flagellants back. The flagellants would continue whipping directly onto the freshly opened abad, aggravating the wounds to a fleshy pulp from which blood would flow even more profusely.

The ritual would begin in earnest in a way that would maintain the sense of horizontal sociality among the gathered men. After a short while, the flagellants would be called to assemble on the nearby pavement, forming a straight line. At this point, the men would have put on blind-folds or long pieces of cloth with eyeholes cut out (some would use balaclavas), tied around the face to preserve anonymity. In unison, the men would strike the burillo on each side of their upper torso, whipping their wounded back repeatedly as they made a five- to six-kilometer walk around the streets of the province. In this sense, the limbon is engaged in a *lakaran*, a Tagalog word that literally means "to walk." The historian Reynaldo Ileto (1979, 56) has described this as the social personification of Christ's Passion: "A pilgrimage, a mission, an ascent . . . perceived in terms of Christ's example in the pasyon: a lakaran from place to place, to spread the word, a lakaran that knows no turning back and ends in Calvary."

A limbon engaged in a lakaran produces a distinct cacophony, a staccato of rhythmic rattling as the collated pieces of wood of the burillo slap against moist open flesh. While the whipping itself is done on an individual basis, the companions who accompany the limbon are just as crucial in facilitating the ritual. Throughout the lakaran, the sunod bears the responsibility of attending to any needs the flagellant has, or catch them in case they should suddenly feel faint from the self-scourging. Indeed, it is not uncommon for flagellants to be overcome with heat exhaustion or loss of blood, upon which they might collapse on to the ground. The sunod will come to their aid. The entire limbon will stop at this point, though the other flagellants will continue their rhythmic striking from a stationary position, resuming only when the flagellant has sufficiently recovered with the help of his sunod. Depending on the route chosen by the men beforehand, the limbon will make stops at makeshift house altars, called *puni*, where the flagellants will lie spread-eagled on the ground, seemingly deep in prayer. As if on cue, the sunod begins to wallop the flagellant's buttocks and lower thighs—as hard as he was able, so it seemed—with wads of old newspapers rolled up into solid rods. After a few strikes, the flagellants continue their journey, at which point the wounds on their backs will have taken on the distinctive shape of a large red heart, moist and glimmering in the afternoon sun.

Partaking in a flagellant group, one cannot help but feel implicated in the vibrancy of group machismo as bonds of friendly camaraderie are reaffirmed. As the ritual progresses into a lakaran, the flagellants are supported by their companions, who take on different modes of ritual facilitation: from a berdugo, who is literally responsible for the flow of blood that gives self-flagellation its gruesome character, to a sunod, who is crucial to ensuring that flagellants maintain the physical composure to complete the lakaran. Having said that, the formation of horizontal group dynamics is not the only purpose of ritual agency among practitioners. Having discussed the mechanics of pagdarame, in what follows, I take a more detailed look at individual flagellants to examine the notion that self-flagellation is concerned with the cultivation of a multisubjective relationship of empathy.

Conventional Empathy

The concept of "empathy" is defined as the human capacity to understand, relate to, and share the subjective experience of others, involving a sentimental "reading" of a body outside of ourselves. This intersubjective reading is premised upon specific subject positions that are often circumstantial.

Typically, the empathic subject seeks to imagine the experience of another's situation. According to nursing studies scholar Theresa Wiseman (1996, 1164) empathy differs from sympathy in that "we try to imagine what it is like being that person and experiencing things as they do, not as we would."

There is an impressive amount of philosophical discourse to suggest that humans have an innate capacity to detect and meaningfully interpret the inner states of others. Philosopher of the mind Karsten Stueber (2010, 5) argues that empathy is the "epistemically central, default method for understanding other agents." In the hermeneutic tradition, the capacity to inhabit another person's point of view is understood as a facet of our visceral understanding (*verstehen*) of other minds, or of fostering an interpretive hypothesis about others. In confronting the "problem of other minds," the German philosopher Theodore Lipps (1903) described empathy as the human tendency to perceive other people's emotional states from their facial and bodily gestures, upon which kinesthetic "sense-feelings" are mirrored in the observer through a process of "inner imitation." Similarly, the phenomenological position represented by Edmund Husserl ([1913] 1970) and Edith Stein ([1917] 1964) saw empathy as an engagement with an interlocutor—a minded being—who is within the realm of one's direct perceptual observation. The phenomenologist Maurice Merleau-Ponty (1964, 52–53) put it thus: "Anger, shame, hate and love are not psychic facts hidden at the bottom of another's consciousness: they are types of behavior or styles of conduct which are visible from the outside. They exist on this face or in those gestures, not hidden behind them."

Beyond philosophy, scholars from a variety of disciplines, including clinical and social psychology, neuroscience, primatology, sociology, and anthropology, have discussed how humans are attuned to one another's inner states, in all societies and varying circumstances, through the observation of affective states (for a summary of this research, see Hatfield, Cacioppo, and Rapson 1994). More recent advances in the neurosciences have identified mirror neurons that are part of an ensemble of sensory and perceptual mechanisms. Bioethicist Jodi Halpern (2001) has demonstrated that humans are neurophysiologically attuned to "read" and respond to mental states manifested in the outwardly observable physical responses of the human body: the contortions of the face, the tone of the voice, or mannerisms and gestures.

Social science and theological research on cross-cultural settings would seem to corroborate the embeddedness of empathy on the perception of bodily affect. A very useful synthesizing analysis of human sensation (in particular, pain) and its communicative function is provided by theology scholar Ariel Glucklich (1998, 390), who perceptively argues that a reductive psychological theory, while useful, "fails miserably to account for the phenomenological voice of participants who undergo pain." The anthropologist C. Jason Throop's observations among the Yapase indicate that a specific bodily response, *so ulum* (goose bumps), provides empathic cues to discern the emotions of other people (Hollan and Throop 2011, 15). Collectively, what the research suggests is that empathy is not just a matter of projecting subjective inner states onto another but is based on the physiologically hardwired inclination to associate inner states with the instinctive outward bodily externalization of emotions.

What a cross-cultural perspective further contributes to our understanding of empathy is the sense that bestowing empathy implies one's position of relative competency, and even higher status, about the subject of empathy (Hollan and Throop 2011, 14). The anthropologist Elfriede Hermann (2011, 32) observes that among the Banban of Fiji, the empathizer possesses a special capacity to show pity for others such that the self "is socially and economically better positioned vis-à-vis the stranger (or traveler), who is solitary and needy. This implies, despite the points of sameness, the existence of a hierarchy between where they are positioned and where he is." The notion that there is a sense of hierarchy in the empathic relationship is very significant in our understanding of pagdarame, which, as I shall show in the rest of the chapter, is an empathy between several subjects who occupy different and paradoxically unequal positions in the ritual frame.

Triangulated Empathy

The research that I have outlined above shows that empathy is most intuitively understood as an intersubjective, two-way relationship between two individuals who, in sharing time and place, cultivate emotions of consociation in the reading of each other's bodily cues and affects. The crafting of a connection between empathizer and suffering subject/s is not, in and of itself, the end result of pagdarame. In the ritual expression of pagdarame, the empathetic relationship is one triangulated between a self-flagellant, who is the empathizer, and two other subjectivities: Christ, who was crucified, and someone close to the empathizer who is, in various ways, suffering. The end result of this triangulation is not the mere expression of consociation but a material change in the circumstances of the third subject, an outcome that is predicated upon embodying suffering onto painful ritual practices. Since pagdarame is most commonly premised upon the medical predicament of the third subject, empathy is seen as a way to address the circumstances necessitated by the limits of biomedicine.

The triangulated empathy that is channeled by ritual practitioners is, in effect, an appeal for Christ (as the second subject of empathy) to validate the commensurability between the empathizer's pain and his worthiness to receive divine intervention for the material benefit of a suffering third party. Looking deeper into individual motivations of self-flagellants themselves, it is common for triangulated empathy to be a facet of a sense of material providership, as flagellants seek to address the prevailing misfortunes and circumstances of their loved ones. Pagdarame, in this sense, places ritual practitioners in a position of empowerment, where they can act to affect the predicament of those others who suffer.

This is an empowerment, however, that has two very important, even paradoxical, caveats. First, triangulated empathy can be framed only upon the empathizer's lowering himself to a subordinate position of humility and vulnerability, particularly in relations to Jesus, who is simultaneously a subject of pity. It is in this way that pagdarame is uniquely paradoxical form of empathy. Ritual agents (the flagellant), as well the subject of empathy (the suffering Christ) are both empowered and vulnerable at the same time. Flagellants are empowered to facilitate ritual intentions even while they channel a vulnerable position. Christ, meanwhile, is suffering to the point of death (the Passion) even while he is empowered to grant the flagellant's request.

To the extent that this paradoxical empathic relationship seeks an end result that is God's favorable intervention, those who perform pagdarame can be considered supplicants in the conventional sense of the word. To "supplicate," from Latin *supplicare*, meaning "to kneel down," is to make a humble appeal, typically in the form of prayer, to a superior other who has the power to grant a particular request. Pagdarame channels a supplicatory agency that is an intuitive, faith-driven connection with God, in this case, understood and imagined as the suffering Christ. A magdarame devotes ritual action toward God, while acknowledging that God will respond according to a higher wisdom or laws of divine dispensation, which may not follow the conventional logic of reciprocation.

At the same time, pagdarame can be seen as a ritual in which one takes on an intermediary role that is more conventionally conducted by the pantheon of saints. The concept of "intercession" emphasizes the role of a third party (in Christian theology, normally the Virgin Mary or the Saints) who are invoked because they have a special capacity to advocate for God's grace on behalf of another person. Intercession is cultivated as a linear, vertical mode of interaction with divine superiors, evoking the "communion of saints" as the spiritual solidarity that binds people with the souls in purgatory, and the saints in heaven, who are all part of the mystical body under Jesus.

The supplicant-intermediary role of the flagellant is more interesting considering that darame is an empathic relationship that is entered into under conditions of imperfect perception. After all, a flagellant cannot directly perceive another's pain or fully understand God's wisdom of reciprocation. How can empathy be crafted without direct experience of another's predicament? How can empathy be framed under circumstances of divine inscrutability? We turn now to these two aspects of empathy triangulated in the ritual pursuit of pagdarame.

Empathic Humility

The empathy that is channeled in pagdarame is not just about pain but also about crafting and emphasizing a sense of humility relative to Jesus. This was explained to me by Masu (or "Cap," as he is known), the village headman of San Pedro Cutud, who has been in a position to observe flagellants for most of his life. Like many others in the province, Cap described pagdarame as *penitensya* (literally, "doing penitence"): "[Self-flagellants] do penitence so that God will not think that they are too proud," he said, "or else, their pagdarame will be useless!" In the Catholic Encyclopedia (1936), "penitence" is defined as a judicial process of a person showing sorrow and regret for having made a transgression, thereby evoking the desire to seek forgiveness from God through a priest who conducts the sacrament of confession. Far from showing a commitment to sacramental adherence, however, the penitensya of pagdarame underscores a devotional paradox of triangulated empathy, one in which a self-flagellant seeks to render himself vulnerable to the object of his pity. Pagdarame as penitence is less about seeking penance and sacramental absolution than it is about a public channeling of humility to solicit Jesus' favor.

In elaborating upon this sense of humility, Cap drew my attention to the example of a man named Emerito, who in 1995 took his three sons, aged seven, eight, and ten, to perform their pagdarame. Emerito, himself a former self-flagellant, was a manabad, or a person who inflicted deep cuts on the backs of Holy Week self-flagellants at the start of their lakaran. By cutting deep, sharp incisions onto the backs of his sons, Emerito was helping embody their faith (salpantaya king Ginu) that God would cure their loved ones of various health conditions. In 2013, one of the boys, Reggie, who was then twenty-eight, told reporters that he and his brothers had gone on to perform pagdarame for fifteen consecutive years: "We were just kids," he said, "we had nothing, but we wanted to help our kin. We think self-flagellation was the best way to ask God for help" (Orejas 2013).

The participation of "magdarameng anak" (literally, "flagellant children") is not new or even particularly uncommon. A prominent feature of the public sphere of Holy Week is the spectacle of children being socialized in painful rituals (see Bräunlein 2009, 908; Zialcita 2000). Indeed, it came as somewhat of a surprise to me when Cap nonchalantly admitted that he himself was magdarameng anak, who himself started pagdarame at the age of twelve. Like Reggie, Cap took up the ritual as a way to appeal to Jesus to help his paralyzed father. To be sure, his extended family was well-to-do enough to provide support for hospital treatment. Nevertheless, Cap still thought it necessary to perform a sense of humility in the face of his lack of any other means of familial providership: "It was the only way I could help my dad, since I was too young to earn [an income]," he explained.

Aside from magdarameng anak, this aspect of humility in triangulated empathy is demonstrated as well in considering what I have described as "export-quality martyrs" (Bautista 2015). Miguel is a twenty-eight-year-old laborer who was a self-flagellant for over seven years before taking up work as an overseas Filipino worker (OFW). Miguel, along with several other men, was hired by a large car dealership in Saudi Arabia but had at times conflicted with his employer and some of the Saudi workers. "They were arrogant," he said, "and didn't appreciate how I could do things in a creative way [diskarte]." This situation made his job extremely tense, as he was constantly high-strung. But he persevered and concentrated on his work because he "needed to show my family that I was [a capable man] . . . that I could withstand the hard times, that I was strong enough to sacrifice." Miguel pointed to the actual, physical practice of ritual itself as that which offered him the means for engaging in the challenges of work. "[My Saudi employers] didn't know it," he said, "but I'd done self-flagellation for years. Can they do that? My buddies know it, and that gives me confidence to bear the hardship of the job."

Miguel's transnational experience, like that of the magdarameng anak, was one that the anthropologist Maya Mayblin (2014, 342–343) would call "quieter, less bloody forms" of sacrifice. Having performed the rituals of self-flagellation was a source of silent strength, one that was affirmed, at least to Miguel's companions ("my buddies know it"), his "hegemonic masculine privilege" (S. McKay 2011). Miguel admitted that while he did not confront his employers outright, he did bear some ill will toward them, which was a transgression for which he felt a sense of regret. It is this regret that is channeled when he performs pagdarame as a form of *penitensya*: "I know I had ill will [sama ng loob] toward [my Saudi coworkers]," he said, "but I still hope that Jesus will still recognize my penitence and help our family." Admitting to his state of sinfulness in the course of self-flagellation is a way of positioning himself as the flawed appellant of Christ, even while the ritual act itself is an expression of an empathic relationality with the latter's suffering.

One thing that we learn from the experience of Reggie, Cap, and Miguel is that the practice of pagdarame will continue for as long as children in Pampanga, particularly boys, are brought up to internalize an association between ritual action and the formation of masculine identity. In the performance of pagdarame, the body-in-pain is seen as a way for a young person to craft traditional providership roles for the family, even where (at least in the case of Cap) there was no shortage of material resources. Pagdarame is premised upon a paradoxical positioning of the second subjectivity—Christ himself—as an object of empathy who nevertheless can effect a positive change in the circumstances of the empathizer and another suffering subject. Rather than establishing the status of the self-flagellant as a superior empathizer, pagdarame operates more as a channeling of relative humility toward subjects of empathy by admitting to a flawed subjectivity and potential beneficiary of divine favor.

Opacity and Divine Inscrutability

The research on empathy generally construes empathetic agents as sensory beings that "read" other minds by detecting emotional or affective cues among those who share intersubjective time and space. The possibility of empathy is problematized, however, by what anthropologists Joel Robbins and Alan Rumsey (2008) have called "the opacity of other minds," the fact that we cannot really know what others are thinking and feeling. Similarly, the empathy channeled in pagdarame presents a challenge to conventional empathy in that the empathy of the flagellant is not premised upon the actual or direct observation of the recognizable emotional or physical or mental states of others. Pagdarame is a relationship that is crafted between the empathizing self-flagellant and two other subjectivities whom he cannot directly perceive or fully understand. In being blindfolded, for example, the self-flagellating subject pursues ritual agency amid a diminished, if not completely nullified, visual capacity. But in a larger sense, pagdarame is conducted without the copresence of the self-flagellants empathetic interlocutors. How can empathy be possible under these conditions, in which there is no full epistemic access to the minds or bodily affect of the subjects of empathy?

The answer was explained to me by Allan Navarro, in his fifties, who had taken to self-flagellation as a teenager in order to appeal for the recovery of his brother, Ariel, from a congenital heart defect. What made Allan's desire to self-flagellate even more poignant was that he knew that Ariel's recovery was not possible. What Allan sought through self-flagellation was not a cure per se but a way to enhance of efficacy of conventional medicine's palliative effect, as he explained, in recalling why he first performed pagdarame: "I spoke to my brother, and told him that you must get well, even though deep inside I knew that it would only be a matter of time. . . . He is suffering, just like Jesus did, so I thought that doing [pagdarame] would help . . . so that in my [pagdarame], somehow, medicines would help him, even just a little."

It is significant that Allan's empathetic relationship with Ariel is not premised upon full epistemic access to the latter's suffering experience, or even to his emotions. After all, Ariel was frequently in the hospital and would not be present when Allan performed his self-flagellation. Allan's understanding of Ariel's condition is different from the concept of understanding (verstehen) typically associated with empathy, which the German historian J. G. Droysen describes thus: "On being perceived, an expression, by projecting itself into the inner experience of the percipient, calls forth the same inner processes. Thus, on hearing the cry of anguish we feel the anguish of the person who cries and so on" (Droysen [1893]

2015, 12–13, quoted in Stueber 2010, 11). Allan's empathy for Ariel is achieved, rather, amid an imaginative reflection on the Christ's Passion (that he is "suffering, just like Jesus"). Just as he can "understand" what Jesus must have experienced in being crucified—a truth internalized through a pious upbringing—Allan relates to Ariel's condition of suffering in a way that is not reliant on the two sharing in actual copresence. Contrary to conventional forms, the kind of empathic relationality that Allan embodies in pagdarame is a work of imagination, and not perception, of an unseen interlocutor.

Another facet of this paradoxical empathy with unseen, unfelt, and unequal interlocutors is expressed by Ramon, a thirty-two-year-old odd-job worker, who has been self-flagellant in San Fernando for at least ten years. His wife, Ditas, is a twenty-nine-year-old medical technician who secured a job as a medical administrator in a hospital in the Middle East. While Ramon was faced with diminished means of earning sufficient income, Ditas's administrative skills in the medical industry offered the prospect of higher earning potential overseas. When she is overseas, the couple continue to communicate through Skype and other modes of online communication, of which Ramon says, "I can see how difficult it is for her. Even if she has a smile on her face, I know it's so hard for her to be away."

It is because of this that Ramon continues his act of self-flagellation. For his part, Ramon felt that his own ritual suffering approximated the pain his wife undergoes, constituting an expression of pagdarame with her, who was "martyr-like" in embarking on transnational labor. "It pains me, as a father and as a man, that I can't earn enough for my family. . . . But never mind, I will still contribute in my own way and help her. If God can look favorably on my pagdarame, then I will be able to help support my family. Having God's favor is better than money, right?"

There was an awareness that Ditas's working overseas reformulated the traditional roles of financial providership. Through the performance of self-flagellation, Ramon and Ditas reframed sacrifice according to a paradoxical logic of divine reciprocity. In this logic, traditional, gendered means of the generation of familial income are supplanted by an appeal for God to provide due acknowledgment of Ramon's ritual act in the context of his lack of financial capacity. This is a relationship of empathy, however, that is not entered upon with a full knowledge of God's thought process. "We can't really be sure how God will respond to us," reasoned Ramon, "but it is important that I do whatever I can to contribute in my [non-financial] own way."

Pagdarame as triangulated empathy is not just about there being three subjects in the empathic relationship. In essence, it is premised upon an acknowledgment of and appeal to divine omnipotence mediated by the sense that Christ can act as a reciprocating benefactor even while recognizing his suffering and vulnerability . The basis of reciprocation is not transactional rationality—an eye for an eye—but is premised upon the inscrutability of divine prerogative ("We can't really be sure how God will respond"). Even if there is a sense that God is not always a rational agent (since at times he does not grant requests even when rituals are performed), there is a constant and unequivocal belief in the primacy of divine wisdom. It is a paradoxical divine wisdom, moreover, that is maintained even in the course of the Passion ordeal, where the suffering of Christ underscores his capacity to bestow divine favor.

The Empathy of Suffering

In evoking the historian Vicente Rafael, the anthropologist Fenella Cannell (1995, 389) has argued that Filipinos reconstruct their religious commitments, including those otherwise cultivated in formal liturgical contexts, as "opportunities for the creation of (asymmetrical) two-way relations of reciprocity with a social superior." At first blush, this might seem an apt description of the kinds of relationships sought by magdarame, who seek through self-flagellation a way to corporeally manifest their traditionally defined duties of care for one's family, both as an expression of piety and as a source of the strength of spiritual fortitude. The "(asymmetrical) two-way relations of reciprocity" occurs when God bestows positive benefit as a response to the ritual practitioner's pious commitments, even while the latter acknowledges one's unworthiness to receive it.

In this chapter, however, I have channeled my specific ethnographic encounters with self- flagellants in Pampanga to demonstrate that pagdarame is more complicated than this. I have sought to provide conceptual nuance to the notion of reciprocal relationships by situating empathy as the essence of ritual agencies in Pampanga. In conducting pagdarame, the empathizer (that is, the self-flagellant) takes on a multifaceted subject position in relation to two other subjectivities that he expresses empathy for. In channeling this kind of triangulated ritual empathy, a magdarame is both a supplicant and an intercessor in the pursuit of immanent well-being for oneself and those he holds dear. In this sense, pagdarame imbues conventional forms of divine intercession with aspects of ritual interiority that exceed theological or scriptural prescriptions, and evokes more intimate modes of divine communion.

The Way of the Cross
Nailing and the Ritualization of Trust

E very Good Friday, on an empty plot of land on the outskirts of the village of San Pedro Cutud, a small group of local residents reen-act the crucifixion and death of Jesus Christ on a purpose-built mound of dust and ash. A man who plays the title role of Kristo performs lines from a script called the *Via Crucis* (Way of the Cross), which has remained largely unchanged since it was first written over half a century ago. It would not be far-fetched to say that the Via Crucis is witnessed by tens of thousands of spectators, while many thousands more view it from the reports of the major news networks, who each have crews on site. Steel barriers are erected to demarcate the throng of spec-tating masses from an assemblage of celebrities, political heavyweights, and foreign dignitaries. The receptive thousands do not brave the searing afternoon sun to witness a performance of theatrical virtuosity. They come in anticipation of the play's final act of confronting realism, when men dressed as Roman centurions forcibly drag Kristo up to a mound where he is stripped, mocked, and forced face-down to the ground before literally nailing him to a cross. There is no doubt that the Kristo experi-ences extreme pain at the point of nailing, even as he is hoisted up for all the audience to watch aghast.

In this chapter, I discuss this theatrical event of ritual nailing on the cross, or *pamamaku king krus* (*pamamaku* for short) as it unfolds in and through the performance of the Via Crucis Passion play. It is, to be sure, an expression of pious religiosity in which ritual actors seek to cultivate a special kind of relationship with God in and through their participation in various facets of the performance. Beyond this, I am also interested in the circumstances, both institutional and personal, that can help explain the continued performance of this ritual over the past half-century. Do the most commonly held assumptions about the rituals—which range from them being manifestations of fanatic literalism to trance-induced con-frontations with mystic forces—correspond to how ritual actors explain their motivations?

Given that the rituals depict the literal form of the Passion story's climax, it may well be intuitive for any keen observer to relate these inquiries to the pious ideals encapsulated in Thomas A Kempis' *The Imitation of Christ* (1494), a book so influential that it has been described as "the best-loved book of Christianity, after the Bible" (Chadwick 1999, xviii). Kempis extolled the virtue of withdrawal from worldly pursuits, entailing the diminishing of interior states as a way to address the temptations of vanity, materialism, pride, and greed. But more than just a form of ascetic seclusion, imitative self-mortification such as what we witness in pamamaku king krus is commonly associated with a desire for the obliteration of one's sense of selfhood and an overlaying of another. For example, religious studies scholar Ariel Glucklich argues that in the case of voluntarily inflicted ritual pain, "as the self is dismantled, something else gets built up . . . you come to think of yourself not as Jack or Joe, but as Jesus himself, or as Murugan himself. So building the object of devotion, and undermining subjectivity" (Glucklich 2009). This argument resonates with that of literary critic Elaine Scarry, who wrote what is arguably the most prominent analysis of the nature of pain and its effect on human subjectivity, *The Body in Pain: the Making and Unmaking of the World* (1985). In the blurb for this critically acclaimed book, Scarry emphasizes how pain "actively destroys language, reducing sufferers in the most extreme cases to an inarticulate state of cries and moans." In her analysis of various kinds of pain experiences, Scarry has vividly depicted the innate capacity of intense physical pain to break down, and even completely annihilate, the sufferer's sense of self.

As I indicated earlier, a survey of feature articles and opinion pieces in the major Filipino broadsheets in both Tagalog and Kapampangan since the 1960s reveals a prevalent continuance of this theme: that ritual crucifixion is primarily about a form of painful imitation at the expense of the sufferer's own sense of self. In a National Geographic Channel documentary titled *Taboo: Tests of Faith* (Abraham 2002), for example, religious studies professor Yvonne Chireau interprets crucifixion rituals in Pampanga as "giving up oneself. . . . One tends to think that you lose power in giving up the self, but for the religious person it's the opposite: you are embracing something that is greater than yourself, and you are giving up self in order to become powerful."

Yet of all the spectacular and performative aspects of these crucifixion rituals, the most intriguing is how the stated reason for why it is performed is almost completely at odds with what is generally assumed to motivate it. Most, if not all ritual nailees, or *namamaku*, that I have spoken with are adamant that a loss or denial of the self is far from their minds in the performance of the ritual. Instead, a reiteration of their subjectivities—of their personalities, circumstances, emotions and intentions—becomes all the more prominent in the act of ritual nailing. In this chapter, therefore, I do not just seek to describe how extreme pain is meaningful, and in that sense bearable. I also seek to discuss the various institutional, cultural, and even economic reasons that contribute to a ritual in which suffering reiterates the sense of self, particularly in relation to others in the ritual frame.

In the first part of this chapter, I discuss how the Via Crucis has become, over a span of at least three decades, embedded in larger bureaucratic, governmental, and socioeconomic forces, thereby raising it from a small-town affair to an international spectacle. What we witness every Holy Week is a ritual that is embedded in a government-sanctioned and corporate-endorsed program called the Maleldo ("Holy Days"), which emphasizes promoting a theatrical aesthetic rather than cultivating the very personal religious agencies of its main protagonists. This is significant because, as I will show, the first pamamaku in the Via Crucis would not have even been possible were it not for the enactment of personal ritual intentions, particularly in person-to-person relationships of trust (*tiuala*) shared by ritual protagonists and ritual facilitators.

The analytical turn that I take in the next section—something of a corrective to the "neglect of ritual agency" that came with the growth of the Via Crucis—draws from an approach by the anthropologist of Latin America Susanna Rostas, who made a distinction between "performativity" and "ritualization" (Rostas, cited in Hughes-Freeland 1998, 85–104). Whereas "performativity" refers to ritual actions done in relation to an audience, ritualization is conducted without cognizance of spectators (nor even conscious of its own ritual agency, as in ritual trance). I thus sharpen the focus to examine the microritualizations that occur within the spectacle of Via Crucis, and argue that the performativity of the play does not ultimately undermine its meaningfulness as a pursuit of an embodied ritual agency. For this, we consider the perspectives, life stories, and narratives of modern-day namamaku (ritual nailees), the inheritors of the tradition began a few decades earlier, who commonly describe the act in terms of interiorized expressions vow fulfillment, or *panata*. As a channeling of panata, I will show how pamamaku manifests forms of asymmetrical reciprocity and, once again to evoke the origins of the Via Crucis, the channeling of person-to-person trust that facilitates leaps of faith.

At the close of the chapter, I discuss the pamamaku events that occur outside the formal spaces of the Maleldo to demonstrate the extension of ritual agencies in terms of geography and gender. I depict in particular my ethnographic encounters with three namamaku: Jackson Cunanan, who conducted pamamaku in the town of San Vicente, and Lucy Reyes and Percy Valencia, two of the prominent female healer-namamaku in the neighboring province of Bulacan.

Origins: The Albularyo Kristo and *Tiuala*

Rituals of nailing (pamamaku king krus) in central Luzon can be traced back to the year 1955, when Ricardo Navarro, an employee of the Philippine National Railways, wrote and staged a play he called *Via Crucis o Pasyon y Muerte* (The Way of the Cross, the Passion and death). It was a Passion play, or *sinakulo,* that sought to involve everyone in Ricardo's hometown

of San Pedro Cutud (Cutud for short) in the dramatization of Christ's crucifixion. Ricardo was not a formally trained playwright by any means,
and he would not be able to conscript professional thespians or actors for
the production. Instead, he drew upon his own personal finances for the
stage and props, and assigned cast roles to his close family, neighbors,
and friends. What his Via Crucis offered was a way to reorient the townsfolk's collective focus away from gambling and other vices and back to
their religious and spiritual obligations. He did not intend for the play to be
consumed by an audience larger than his immediate vicinity, and could
never have imagined that this small-town affair—a play they could proudly
call Cutud's own—would, in less than half a century, grow to be a spectacle of national and international fascination drawing tens of thousands
of spectators every year.

It was not entirely uncommon for relatively well-to-do local elites such
as Ricardo to facilitate town performances, particularly in Central Luzon,
which has a rich tradition of vernacular theatre.[1] To be sure, there were
many other famous Passion plays performed in Pampanga in the 1950s,
such as the *Misteru ning Kalbaryu* and *Pasion y Muerto,* which featured
actors in the title role of Kristo being tied to the cross with a rope in the
final climax. Theatre scholars Nikki Serranilla-Briones (2010) and Doreen
Fernandez (1996) have observed that such forms of communal theatre are
opportunities to enact personal religious obligations, and that theatre is
"part of the rural lifestyle, and reflective of—and influential on—the
people's worldview" (Fernandez 1996, 12). The performing arts industry
grew a pool of homegrown actors, playwrights and directors. From
Pampanga, according to the Center for Kapampangan Studies, "hundreds
of [productions] were presented . . . within a three-decade period, considered the golden age of Kapampangan drama" (CKS 2002, 13). For the first
five years in which Ricardo's Via Crucis was performed, it did not stand
out from the other more professionally produced plays in the area. But, as
Ricardo's fifty-year old grandson Allan now tells the story, that was about
the change.

Just before the start of Holy Week in 1960, Ricardo's wife fell ill. As was
their custom, the Navarros sought the assistance of both conventional
medicine and that of an *albularyo* (faith healer). This is how Allan told the
story to me in 2012:

> I remember the time when my grandmother got sick, and of course,
> medical doctors [*doktor-doktor*] were scarce, so we consulted an albu-
> laryo first. My father had heard of one called Temyong from Apalit, and
> we sent for him right away. When he came and saw my grandmother,
> he told me to "fetch two eggs," which I did, and then he said, "Fill a
> bucket with water." While I was doing this, I noticed that he began
> whispering something into a little piece of old paper. A few moments
> later, he said to my grandmother, "When the two eggs stand upright in

the water, you will be healed." So she placed the eggs into the water and, yes, they stood up on the water, then she also stood up and was healed.

The point of Allan telling me this story was not to extoll the superiority of the albularyo over conventional medicine. Rather, it was to highlight the close bond that was to develop between Temyong and the Navarro family—a bond of trust (*tiuala*) that was to significantly alter the performance of his grandfather's Via Crucis, and indeed of the entire town's destiny for many years to come. For it was because of this tiuala that Temyong was emboldened to make a serious request in the months to follow. Temyong asked Ricardo that he himself be allowed to play the part of Kristo in the Via Crucis, except that he would not simply be tied to the cross, like all the other actors. As an "albularyo Kristo," Temyong wanted to be nailed.

Nailing someone to the cross, in public, in the context of the Via Crucis was a prospect that had every member of the Navarro household "very very startled." But looking back in hindsight, Temyong's reasons were, as Allan narrated, fairly understandable to Ricardo. It was simply a way for Temyong to maintain and enhance his capacities as an albularyo healer. For Temyong had been trying for many years to acquire a magical stone from the highlands of Mount Banahaw, a sacred mountain frequented by shamans and spirit mediums in the area. This stone, once acquired, would augment an albularyo's healing prowess and thereby facilitate his ambition of becoming a renown religious leader. However, each time he had gotten close to the stone, he had always been thwarted in his attempts by "an invisible kick" that sent him hurtling down the mountain. Year after year, Temyong had embarked upon this quest, but to no avail. He promised to have himself nailed to the cross, in the hope that God would allow him to acquire the stone, thereby accessing the magical properties he believed it contained. "But to do that," Allan maintained, "[Temyong] needed ritual companions who he could have tiuala in, so that he's safe, and [so that] his ritual can have maximum impact."

And so it was that on Good Friday in 1962, two years after he had healed Mrs. Navarro, Temyong became the first man in recorded history to be ritually nailed to the cross in San Pedro Cutud. The "albularyo Kristo" would, in fact, be the first in a long line of men and women who would undergo ritual nailing, or pamamaku king krus. Being the first namamaku (nailee) is no small feat. Although self-inflicted pain through self-flagellation was a well-known practice, Ricardo and his townsfolk knew of no precedent for nailing, and no one had any knowledge of how it was to be carried out without threatening the life of the namamaku. As Allan narrated, Temyong had pioneered the actual method of pamamaku king krus, mobilizing the group in fulfilling specific tasks: "He knew exactly what to do. [Demonstrating with his own palms:] he would pierce his own palms to make a hole to guide us . . . then he would ask us to tie him up on the cross, and we would only need to tap the nail with hammer a few times through the hole he had already made. . . . There would be lots of blood, and you could tell that he was really wounded." All throughout this process, Temyong would be reciting the lines of the Via Crucis, performing it with dramatic effect even while he was orchestrating his own nailing. "He was really good at dramatic performance. . . . He really shouted his lines," says Allan, "but I guess it's because like Jesus, he was really in pain."

In the years after his first nailing, Temyong repeated his performance for at least three more years, each time improving the methodology of nailing. In 1965, Ricardo accepted an invitation for the Via Crucis to be performed in the nearby town of Betis on Holy Thursday, with Temyong nailed again the following day in San Pedro Cutud on Good Friday. This 1965 performance of double nailing was the first time that the Via Crucis caught the attention of the wider provincial media.

Temyong continued to pursue the magic stone from Mount Banahaw, but still to no avail, even in the years after his retirement from the Via Crucis. The albularyo Kristo never acquired the stone, and finally succumbed to illness and old age. By the time he passed away, on Good Friday of April 1993, the event of ritual nailing was well and truly on the way to becoming a national and international spectacle. The Via Crucis grew in prominence year after year, catapulting all those who would play Kristo to the heights of a dazzling, if unintended, stardom.

Suffering as Theatrical Genre

It is reasonable to assume that the fascination for the Kristos who perform pamamaku in central Luzon manifests a preexisting appetite for, and sellability of, the genre of holy suffering. The anthropologist Nicholas Barker has described this in terms of the "non-participatory revival" of the practice from as early as the 1950s leading up to the time that Temyong and Ricardo's Via Crucis was gaining notoriety. Self-mortification featured as a motif in many renown paintings, most notably by internationally acclaimed Kapampangan painter Galo Ocampo in the 1950s, and in the depictions and illustrations of cartoonist Rod Dayao and painter Jose V. Blanco in the decades the followed (Barker 1998, 13). The genre of holy suffering was further propagated in the print media, where the 1960s saw several instances of sensationalist promotion of the "awesome and barbaric" nature of the Passion rituals in major metropolitan dailies, such as *Mabuhay* and *Malaya*. From the 1970s onward, images and evocations of self-mortifying penitents featured strongly in a diverse array of artistic production, literature, and performance. In cinema, for example, the motif of self-flagellation features in Kidlat Tahimik's 1977 *Mabangong Bangunot* (Perfumed nightmare), one of the most celebrated films among film critics even today. Barker (1998, 14) argues that these cultural productions were "deliberately packaged as high art for consumption by Manila's literati, [self-mortification] was once again endorsed as a viable cultural expression of national identity." He makes an interesting distinction between pamamaku and self-flagellation in claiming that while the former was amenable to being appropriated as a national cultural heritage, pamamaku "was regarded by the educated elite as unacceptably fanatical, although ironically it was a genuinely new, post-colonial, indigenous ritual performance" (17).

Official publicity and sponsorship of "the experience" of the macabre had a strong influence in the increasing prominence of the actual rituals held in central Luzon. There is evidence from 1961, for example, that as many as two hundred American tourists visited Pampanga under the auspices the Philippine Tourist and Travel Association specifically to observe self-flagellation rituals (Barker 1998, 18). Official government involvement to promote and support nailing events was certainly in place from at least 1973, when the Department of Tourism (DOT) in Manila provided financial support for Holy Week rituals, as well as publicizing the event in the national print and broadcast media. The DOT's newsletter in 1981, as well as other official press releases up until 1988, included pamamaku king krus in their promotional materials.

Just as crucial in increasing the popularity of the rituals was the involvement of corporate capital since at least the early 1990s. The commercial sponsorship made either through direct financial contribution or in kind is one of the most conspicuous indicators of the growth of events such as pamamaku, which are grounded in specific locations that attract a large audience. Barker (1998) has observed that since 1991, for example, either Coke or Pepsi has erected "the welcome" signs and banners, with their corporate logos, on village entrances where pamamaku events have taken place. This has only intensified in recent years with the involvement of a broader spectrum of corporate interests, ranging from telecommunications to confectionary, whose advertising billboards, flyers, and promotional giveaways saturate the crucifixion areas. Since the 1990s, moreover, the collaboration and participation of foreigners as namamaku has increased media attention beyond the Philippines, according to anthropologist Peter Bräunlein (2009). Among the notable ones are the Belgian nun Godelieve Rombaut in 1994, Japanese performer Shinichiro Kaneko in 1996, British performance artist Sebastian Horsely in 2000, and mockumentary filmmakers Dominik Diamond in 2006 and John Safran in 2009.

From Via Crucis to Maleldo

Since Temyong's first nailing in 1962, the Via Crucis has grown tremendously, both in scale and popularity, due at least in part to a fascination with the macabre. The most significant factor in the transition of the Via Crucis from a small-time, private production to international event was its integration into the official programs of municipal government. The best example of this is the Via Crucis' inclusion in the Maleldo, a series of scheduled and formally promoted events made possible through the administrative and logistic provisions of the municipal government of the city of San Fernando, and the wider provincial government of Pampanga province.

Among several events that commemorate Holy Week, by far the biggest draw of Maleldo is the reenactment of Christ's Passion, including the Via Crucis, which culminate in pamamaku done in three official designated areas in the city. The town of San Pedro Cutud, where nailing first took place, had been designated since 2004, while crucifixion events in the nearby towns of San Lucia and San Juan were added in 2008.[2] Among the three towns that receive the government's support, the pamamaku king krus in San Pedro Cutud is the most celebrated, primarily because it is acknowledged as the oldest and most "authentic." It is the Via Crucis that overshadows all other cultural and religious events in the entire province of Pampanga. I was told in 2014 by the head of the municipal tourism board that the Via Crucis seems to be "all that San Fernando is known for during the Maleldo."

Official designation entitles the performers of pamamaku productions such as the Via Crucis to financial, logistical, and medical assistance from the local government. A task force committee comprised of the mayor, the artistic director of the play, tourism and law enforcement officials, and representatives from corporate sponsors is convened every year to coordinate this process. City officials are at pains to point out that they do not interfere with the content of the Passion plays or with the script of the production. Their official mandate, as they see it, is to prevent traffic congestion by managing road closures for the event. An important responsibility of the local headman (*barangay tanod*) is the maintenance of law and order against such incidents as petty crime or, worse, terrorist attacks. Other logistical support includes the provision of public information systems, public amenities, and a first aid station. "If a dignitary is to visit San Fernando," as I was told by a San Fernando city councilor during one of the planning meetings, "it is important that the city government can extend to them the proper courtesies." As it turns out, this mainly includes prime seating in the designated VIP areas during crucifixion events such as the Via Crucis.

These days, government support contributes to the facilitation of the Via Crucis but only to the extent that it can foster a particular kind of theatrical aesthetic. It is a production that involves, to evoke theatre scholar Joachim Fiebach (2002), acts of performative communication with an audience through all-encompassing movements and expressions, and the corresponding use of objects/props/paraphernalia to convey a sense of theatricality. The production involves a cast of about forty local, nonprofessional actors who perform roles based on Ricardo's original 1955 script. With government support, the Via Crucis can be witnessed by anyone, not just local townsfolk, as it unfolds along the five-kilometer route around the streets of San Pedro Cutud, featuring stops in front of various residential homes, each designated as a station in Christ's Passion. Upon arrival at each station, the actors deliver lines committed to memory, their voices amplified by lapel microphones, which transmit wirelessly to several large speakers loaded on to a slow-moving lorry that follows the entire play. After several stations, the play progresses to a purpose-built hill, called a *burol,* at the outer rim of the village where heavy security and strictly regulated restricted zones are enforced by city government officials, the police, and even a SWAT team. By the time the play reaches this stage, as many as twenty to twenty-five thousand spectators (estimate in Barker 1998, 19) would have amassed to witness the climax—the nailing of the lead actor to one of three crosses affixed on the burol.

In what follows, I describe the experience of being part of the government-sponsored, international spectacle that is Via Crucis from the perspective of a cast member–observer, a role I had been granted by the grandson of the writer of the 1955 script and current director of the Via Crucis, Allan Navarro.[3] It is from this vantage point that I seek to convey what it is like to be, as one seasoned Kapampangan journalist put it, "a silent witness to the rare, excruciatingly painful expressions of faith, making Cutud, unofficially, the Calvary of the Philippines" (Orejas 2005).

As the Romans Do: Embedded in the Via Crucis

It is 8:30 in the morning of Good Friday 2011 at the residence of Aling Belen in San Pedro Cutud. Belen, a widower in her fifties, has been a "patron" of the Via Crucis production for many years, and returns to Pampanga from Guam, where she works. Intermittently, a news crew would drop by, each time accompanied by a local guide who was in one way or another related to or acquainted with a person in Belen's household. There are also some foreigners from all parts of the world, who sit together on the porch of Belen's house. There is a heightened sense of excitement and expectation when the Via Crucis' director, Allan Navarro, enters the scene. "Direk Allan," as he is commonly known, is himself in costume, though he is not actually a performer. At this point, in the lead-up to "showtime," he would spend a few minutes here and there talking to the various visitors and reporters. He, like all the other cast members who by now are posing happily for photos with the "privileged" few in the compound, revels in the attention.

I am also in costume: a white habit and a green sash. For I am myself a cast member, a privilege accorded to me by Direk Allan after many days spent interviewing him about the play. My role is that of San Juan, or Saint John the Beloved, to whom the Virgin Mary was bequeathed by Jesus upon his death (I am more than three times mistaken for a foreign priest). As the cast members don their costumes, the mood is jovial and light.

By 10:00 a.m, there are masses of people gathered in the vicinity of the town's Barangay Hall for the main event. There is virtually no crowd control to separate the scores of reporters, filmmakers, bystanders, children, and sunburnt tourists. As they cast moves out of the compound and into the street, Direk Allan orchestrates the play as the actors move around the alleyways and thoroughfares where he himself has spent his entire life. As recently as 2005 there were no amplification facilities. Instead, Direk would repeat Kristo's lines through a megaphone, as a ventriloquist would, for the benefit of the viewing public (Cuyno, Gutierrez, and Takeno 2005). But this year, there is a new addition—wireless microphones, transmitting the voices of the actors to two large speakers on a lorry following behind the actors. Though he himself has no lines, Direk Allan is a dominating presence, barking cues and instructions to the actors, as well as admonishing people to allow some breathing space for his cast. This is not helped by the fact that the play takes place along the narrow streets of Barangay Cutud, which is made even more congested by the number of cars, pedicabs, horse-drawn carriages, and tricycles that line the streets for the occasion.

Soon, the cast reaches the place where I am waiting, at which time the Kristo has already been captured by the Roman centurions, locally known as the *hudjo*. A large wooden cross weighs heavily upon the Kristo's shoulder as he carries it throughout the duration of the street play. Having performed this role for decades, Kristo delivers his lines flawlessly, though the lines are intermittently carried by interruptions to the signal of the wireless microphone. The roman centurions effectively act as crowd control, ensuring that the cast has enough room to perform the scene. This can be achieved only to a limited extent, with the sheer volume of children, spectators, media, and tourists seeking proximity to the action.

Most, if not all, carry some kind of camera or recording device that they attempt to squeeze through a forest of heads and limbs in pursuit of the best shot. In spite of these events, or these distractions, one never gets the sense that Kristo will not be able to continue the journey. Though overcome, he is never really overwhelmed, and picks himself up with no assistance to continue to journey to its completion.

There is a palpable sense of expectation, and not a few cheers, as the Kristo is led by the hudjo from the streets of the village to the crucifixion mound area. He enters bearing the cross that he has carried on his shoulder for several kilometers. Unlike in past years, however, the Kristo will not be nailed to that same cross. Instead, he will be nailed to a wooden cross fastened to a custom-made steel contraption, which contains hinges that fasten it firmly to the ground and allow it to be easily hoisted up from a lying position. After being manhandled and pushed around a few more times, the Kristo is laid on this second cross, where he lies motionless, seemingly deep in thought and prayer. Huddled around him are the centurions, who in reality are the friends he has known for most of his life, and have accompanied him in this performative ritual. Isopropyl alcohol is sprayed onto his outstretched palms and his feet. The nails that are to be used for the Kristo and are extracted from a jar are the same two that have been nailing the Kristo for at least the past five years.

A hudjo stands on each side of the Kristo and they begin inspecting and tracing the exact points at which he will drive the nails into his palms. The first hudjo pushes the nail, firmly and decisively, into that precise point in the Kristo's open palm. The Kristo lets out a moan, audible through the lapel microphone still fastened on him—the shriek of pain that one might have been expecting to occur upon the strike of the hammer. Audiences far from the action would have little clue about this. Once both nails have pierced the Kristo's palms, the centurion takes the hammer and lifts it up with dramatic effect for the crowd to behold. He swings the hammer downward, but the actual strike on the nail is but a quick succession of firm taps. The audience lets out a collective yelp with the strike of the hammer. Kristo too exhales a moan, but not as sharp as at the initial puncture. Each nail is driven through flesh and muscle just deep enough to touch the wood beneath.

The Kristo is then fastened to the cross by a long white cloth that acts both as support and tourniquet. His feet are placed on a wooden foot stand attached near the base of the cross. The hudjo slowly and ceremoniously lift up the cross and, for a few moments, effectively display the Kristo to a rapt, and eerily silent, audience. From this position, the Kristo's feet are nailed one by one between the fleshy parts separating the toes by a centurion on a ladder. The Kristo breathes deeply as he recites his remaining lines. In the final moment, when Christ commits his own spirit to God the Father, the Kristo delivers his speech with more enunciation and volume before he hangs his head forward and breathes his last. After about fifteen minutes, the hudjo move in coordinated fashion to remove the nails simultaneously. Each extraction draws a sigh from Kristo, who seems to "wake up" with each motion. Supported by two other hudjo, he is hoisted down using the cloth rope that had been draped over him on the cross. Meanwhile, the two medical staff bring a stretcher to the cross and take Kristo to the medical recovery tent, where more medics are stationed.

With that, the Via Crucis as a formalized theatrical production ends without so much as a final bow from the cast, and no applause from the crowd. There is no grand exit because the departure of the Kristo is not just the end of the play but the start of a similarly painful ordeal for as many as seventeen other men who have been waiting in the backstage area for their turn to be nailed.[4] These prospective namamaku are not part of the play itself, since they have no lines and do not join the street procession. However, they are part of the spectacle in the sense that they are nailed by the hudjo, three at a time, in front of the audience, which is then allowed through the barricades to watch the nailing in close proximity without any seeming regulation.

Panata: Ruben's Via Crucis

Although as many as seventeen men (and, though far less frequently, women) are nailed following the play's final scene, only one man, Ruben Enaje, can claim to be the "Kristo" of the Via Crucis, having performed the title role for the past three consecutive decades.

Ruben, like most male namamaku in Pampanga, describes the act as a fulfillment of a "panata." When we first met in 2010, Ruben defined "pan-ata" simply as "a vow to repay God for the good things he's done for me." It is not uncommon for both *magdarame* (self-flagellants) and namamaku to relate panata to a petition for God to make a positive future intervention into the life of the petitioner. In the case of Ruben, however, panata is a vow to express a continued sense of thanksgiving for his own salvation from what he thought should have been his own certain death. Here is how he explained the story of how he first decided to conduct pamamaku in 1986:

> My job is to paint large canvas signs, but there were times when I did some work painting high on buildings. I was on this job once in Tarlac in 1985, when I fell from three, four stories high. I remember falling backward towards the ground, and shouted, *"Dios ko po!"* [Oh my God!]. When I landed, I lay there for a few seconds and checked myself. . . . I was completely fine! From that moment, I made a vow to devote [myself to] pamamaku. I thought to myself that the only reason why I was not injured was because of God.

This was the reason for the first nine years of Ruben's pamamaku. The subsequent nine years were devoted to the healing of his daughter, Ejay, from asthma, and the nine years after that, to the recovery of his wife, Juanita, from a throat ailment. Over the years since 2013, there have been several reasons for his ritual act, some concerning the wider political situation of the country, others more to do with his family. In all cases, panata is identified by Ruben as the guiding principle that motivates his ritual agency, and is the main reason he will continue for an unspecified time.

By his own admission, Ruben is not especially gifted or endowed with exemplary spiritual knowledge that would mark him as particularly deserving of divine grace. Indeed it is precisely his lack of distinction that made the fact of God's intervention all the more magnanimous, and made the necessity of his reciprocation even more crucial. Ruben experienced God's grace in the course of his daily toil. There is, in that respect, a certain sense of dignity to his decision to follow Jesus' example. "After all," he says, "Jesus was a humble man too."

Panata, however, cannot be understood as thankfulness or vow fulfillment in the conventional sense. To understand the precise nature of the vows in the context of ritual nailing, Ruben encouraged the understanding of two related concepts, concerning one's interior state, or *lub*: *utang na lub* (literally, a "debt of interiority"), and *tiuala ya lub*.

Asymmetrical Reciprocity and Vow Fulfillment

A particular logic of reciprocity, contained in the concept of panata and *utang na loob* (Miranda 1989, 52), emerges in Ruben's understanding of why he survived his accident and his subsequent motivation to engage in ritual nailing: "I have a great sense of utang na loob to God for saving me when I fell. If not for him, I wouldn't even have the ability to do anything. My crucifixion is my panata, and it doesn't end until I feel God has told me so. I give thanks to the Lord through the example of Jesus."

What Ruben describes here is more complex and nuanced than a simple debt transaction. In describing panata as utang na loob, the terms of vow fulfillment is not a straightforward restoration of parity between two equal, transacting parties. Panata facilitates a specific kind of reciprocity that is based not on an equivalency but on the unquestioned prerogative of one side (God) to determine, and change or prolong the terms of the two-way transaction. In essence, to enact a panata is to create an asymmetrical reciprocity between oneself and the divine, one that the anthropologist Fenella Cannell described as "hierarchical relations [which] are represented as constantly in process, with the subordinate party always drawing in (and drawing towards) the superior, although never entirely closing the gap" (Cannell 1995, 389). There is never really any expectation of a guaranteed result, even after the ritual is performed, and the vow remains outstanding regardless of all attempts by the ritual agent to express thankfulness and gratitude. In this asymmetry, the interiorized expression of gratitude is motivated by the perpetual deferment, whereby the time frame is always open for reevaluation by the superior party in the relationship. Indeed, Ruben seems at peace with a tacit acceptance that his panata will be prolonged indefinitely, for so long as God "wants me to keep doing it, even if I don't understand why."

It is significant, moreover, that Ruben says, "I give thanks to the Lord through the example of Jesus." Here, a distinction is made between God the Father and his Son, yet in such a way that assumes that Ruben's embodied engagement with the latter (that is, his ritual nailing) may go some way toward eliciting the good favor of the former. Having said that, Ruben is quick to point out that the physical ordeal of the pamamaku can never be equal to Christ's Passion, neither in the severity of pain nor in its soteriological significance. No matter how much pain, how much anguish, how much sacrifice Ruben goes through, it will never surmount Christ's own experience. And this is why, he tells me, he cannot simply stop performing in the Via Crucis, and that "it doesn't end until I feel God has told me so."

Panata, then, is premised on the absolute discrepancy between a *mamamaku*, "an ordinary man," as Ruben would describe himself, and God as the supreme deity. *Pamamaku* was deemed to be the only possible act that could approximate a meaningful response to the sheer magnitude of God's magnanimous compassion toward an underserving beneficiary.

While uang na loob is a key sentimental concept in explaining Ruben's motivations for both panata and pamamaku, the mechanics of the ritual action is premised on the micro-ritualizations that occur within the theatrical frame. It is to the significance of trust in the performance of religious agency that we turn to next.

Trusting Faith: Tiuala ya Lub

The reciprocity that is addressed in panata can only be fulfilled through the ritual facilitation of others. To an extent greater than the other members of the cast, Ruben's ritualization is predicated upon the *entrustment of ritual agency* to others who co-inhabit the ritual frame. Ruben emphasized themes of trust in his fellow cast members, who he calls *catiuala,* or literally "cotrusted." According to Ruben, "I get through [my panata] every year because I have trust [tiuala ya lub] in Direk and those who nail me. They know how to nail me properly, and [because] they have good timing."

Ruben conveyed two aspects of tiuala ya lub as it pertains to pamamaku. First of all, nailing is possible because of his confidence in the capacity of certain cast members to facilitate his ritual action in a way that is technically effective (they "know how to nail") and synchronous ("they have good timing") with the larger theatrical aesthetic and flow of the Via Crucis production. These are technical proficiencies that must be deployed in a way consonant with the theatrical frame—that is, a catiuala is not simply anyone who is an expert in the use a hammer, or even one who is medically trained in safety protocols, but "they also have to know the script so that they know *when* to use [the hammer]."

The second aspect of tiuala ya lub goes beyond the matter of technical proficiency, evoking what has been described by some scholars of Filipino Roman Catholicism as a sense of "trusting faith or believing trust" (Silos 1985, 32). This is tantamount to a confidence in a complementarity of interior states between the ritual agent and his catiuala. In this very important sense, tiuala ya lub is effectively a volitional extension of one's *interiority,* as indicated by the word "lub"(and in Tagalog as "*loob*"), to a trusted servant or steward (Tantingco 2006, 106). In its simplest usage, "lub" is defined as the inside or interior of something.[5] When thought of in terms of ritual, "lub" refers to someone's attitudes, innermost feelings, and emotions, as well , intellectual, moral, and spiritual dispositions. In emphasizing lub in the context of "trusting faith," Ruben disputes the notion of an impervious interior state. In *A Secular Age*, the philosopher Charles Taylor (2007, 613) described the modern secular condition as composed of "buffered selves" undergoing a process of "excoriation" in which there is a "transfer of our religious life out of bodily forms of ritual, practice and worship, so that [religion] comes to reside more and more 'in the head.' "

For Ruben, however, religious agency is predicated upon a *porosity* of interior states, which involves the outward channeling of inner personhood—that is to say, one's volition and intentionality—toward an intersubjective relationship with a trusted intersubject. This is not just "in the head" but corporeally embodied in the complicit facilitation of pain, both for the nailer who inflicts it, and the nailee who feels it. Ruben's pursuit of panata is a subjectively embodied experience of affect, but one in which his agency is not bounded by the parameters, or the interior "bufferdness," of the human body. He entrusts his agency upon the expectation of corresponding facilitative action on the part of the catiuala. As important as it is to understand utang na loob as a two-party transaction that motivates ritual nailing, it is also significant that there are actually multiple subjects who are complicit in the enactment ritual frame. Pamamaku, in this regard, constitutes panata that is a conjoined ritual embodiment.[6]

The Ritualization of Trust

If there is a sense of poignancy about the pamamaku and the Via Crucis, it is not because of the gruesomeness of its actual enactment. It lies, rather, in the fact of the relatable human elements that motivated it to begin with. For Ricardo Navarro, the writing and staging of the Passion play was driven simply by a sense of civic obligation that was also an expression of his personal relationship to God. For the albularyo Kristo Temyong, engaging in pamamaku was coterminous with the pursuit of efficacy in his craft as a healer. It is true, as I have shown, that Ricardo's small-town play became embedded in larger sociopolitical and economic forces that capitalize on the sellability and economic viability of the genre of suffering. Those with an appetite for the macabre would hardly suspect that an event of such epic proportions as today's Via Crucis began when two very ordinary and otherwise unremarkable village folk had enough trust in each other's ritual commitments that, together in pamamaku, they took a very important leap of faith. What has always remained is the fact that the pamamaku is still a very personal act of piety with very personal ritual motivations that is most meaningfully enacted with the complicity of ritual collaborators.

If there is a sense that Ruben had inherited something from the original Kristo Temyong, it is not simply the right to perform the Via Crucis script and fulfill a highly regarded theatrical persona. It is, rather, the capacity to channel a particular kind of intersubjective relationship, one that extends one's religious agency horizontally to ritual cofacilitators. Like Temyong, who trusted enough in Ricardo's family to perform what was at the time a completely unheard of religious act, Ruben too had the willingness and wherewithal to share what is "inside" of him with his catiuala in order to facilitate his vows to God.

Asymmetrical reciprocity and trusting faith are the underlying conceptual bases for panata, which is channeled and cultivated in the enactment of pamamaku. This might be lost on us if we were to judge purely on the way the nailing is depicted in both the local and international media. It is easy to assume that the Via Crucis is a spectacle aimed primarily at evoking a theatrical aesthetic that derives its impact from a performance of gruesome literalism in the pamamaku. Yet the many who are fascinated by the macabre may perhaps be disappointed that ritual protagonists do not have any special superhuman capacity for pain, nor a divinely bestowed mental fortitude for spiritual transcendence, or even a radical interpretation of theological forms. As Ruben says, he is "just an ordinary man" who has made a vow to repay God's grace.

Ethnographic Encounters

Having described pamamaku king krus in terms of its theatrical origins, and having discussed how reciprocity and trust condition the motivations and facilitations of its practitioners, here I channel the ethnographic encounters I have had with other namamaku in the region in order to depict how ritual agencies extend to nearby towns and villages in the vicinity of San Fernando. In contrast to the large-scale government-sponsored crucifixions of Via Crucis and Maleldo, nailing rituals also occur at relatively lower-scale settings outside of the three officially designated pamamaku sites. It is fair to say that pamamaku in these locations are relatively less spectacular compared to the scale of theatricality we find in the Via Crucis. Indeed, in some cases, the details of which towns are "hosting" pamamaku are publicized only through word of mouth in contrast to the full-fledged advertising campaigns of the Maleldo. Indeed, the relative remoteness of these more low-key pamamaku, as well as the lack of any bureaucratic procedures to influence their enactment, make them an attraction for those who prefer to avoid the congested scenario of Maleldo. In looking at these pamamaku events outside of San Fernando, I look to my encounters with three namamaku in particular: Jackson Cunanan, who conducted pamamaku in the town of San Vicente half an hour from San Fernando, and Lucy Reyes and Percy Valencia—two prominent female healer-namamaku in central Luzon.

Jackson Cunanan

One type of non-Maleldo pamamaku can historically be linked to what Nicholas Barker (1998, 19) has called the "traveling crucifixion circus" from the 1980s, in which certain men would, at the behest of an affluent sponsor, be paid to perform crucifixion dramas in various towns around Luzon. Today it is rare to encounter namamaku who would openly admit to being paid for their performance. Nevertheless, village crucifixions are still held through the patronage of local political elites, who "sponsor" Holy Week events ostensibly for community outreach and enriching religious observance. Unlike those staged under the Maleldo, these pamamaku events focus on the actual nailing itself and do not involve a sinakulo theatrical performance, and there are no rehearsals or peripheral activities before or after the event.

In looking to observe nonofficial pamamaku, I admit that I had all sorts of assumptions before I met Jackson Cunanan, a longtime namamaku in Pampanga. When I first met him in 2009, I was expecting to meet with someone who was extremely pious and even blinded by a fanatic sense of devotion. Perhaps I expected someone who was obsessed with achieving ethical self-mastery through feats of the body: the kind of character frequently featured in the crucifixion documentaries. Indeed, Jackson was the main feature in an Irish documentary titled *Decoding Christianity* (Rooke 2008), which depicted in typically melodramatic detail the ordeal of Passion ritual practitioners in Pampanga. In the documentary, Jackson speaks to the camera as though being interviewed; his voice is overlaid with an ominous soundtrack and the voice of a particularly eloquent interpreter. Though he communicates very effectively in English, he was asked to speak in his native dialect, presumably to capture the "authentic" and exotic flavor of this gruesome ritual act. Documentaries, particularly ones such as this that focus on the macabre and grotesque, have a way of objectifying their subjects to the extent that what we see onscreen is not Jackson as a person but as a caricature of a particular set of exoticized assumptions.

The person I met was polite, deferential, and, in spite of my protestations, always referred to me as "sir." And Jackson did not refer to himself as a "Kristo" but simply as an "ordinary namamaku." In fact, what was interesting about Jackson is how unremarkable he is. At the time we first met, his most recent occupation was as a construction worker on the Diosdado Macapagal International Airport (DMIA) expansion project in Clark Airfield. Though this work kept him extremely busy, it was not a permanent job, and as such he had a lot of anxiety about his longer-term prospects. Though he struck me as a jovial character, he would express a sense of exasperation, particularly when he speaks about matters of faith and religiosity. There is an intensity about him when he explains why he undergoes crucifixion.

Jackson's sense of religious piety is intertwined with his devotion to his family, which is the main consideration that influences his attitude toward the opportunities presented by transnational labor. Jackson first decided to be nailed in 1993, when his wife was diagnosed with poliomyelitis. He did not initially tell his parents about his intention to conduct pamamaku for fear of their disapproval. Although he knew that his parents would likely be present during the crucifixion rituals in their vicinity, he relied on the fact that his face would remain covered and they would not be able to recognize him. He had conducted nailing in this secretive way for every year since 1993.

In 2010, Jackson chose to be nailed in the town of San Vicente on the invitation of the mayor. One could say that San Vicente, in the municipality of Apalit some thirteen kilometers southwest of the provincial capital San Fernando, is among the more obscure towns in the province. Situated along the MacArthur Highway and not having any particular attractions of general interest, it might be said that those who come to San Vicente are either coming home or coming with a purpose. The town's mayor, whose son is running to replace him in the municipal elections, had organized the crucifixion area with a great sense of purpose and intent. Barricades were placed around the site as a means of crowd control (and, as it turned out, media management). A brass band had been commissioned to perform throughout the ritual, playing tunes that ranged from Korean pop songs to crooner ballads. Banners and streamers from the mayor's son's election campaign were displayed prominently for all to see. If that was not enough, all those who were tasked with a role in the ritual, including the nailers, wore campaign T-shirts emblazoned with the name and smiling face of the mayoral hopeful. There was little doubt about who the benefactor of this ritual was.

On the day before the nailing ritual was to take place, a group of three young men had indicated their intention of being nailed along with Jackson, who took it upon himself to evaluate the sincerity of their motivations. This evaluation was not tantamount to an assessment of their level of religious devotion or piety, as would be made by a priest in the sacrament of confession. Rather, as Jackson told me, it was to make sure that they "are not simply there for the notoriety" (nagpapasikat) or, as has been the case in the past, as "an attempt to profit" from a sense of exhibitionism (pume-pera). Some of the men, such as twenty-three-year-old Michael, had previously commemorated Holy Week through self-flagellation. That year marked a "graduation" of sorts to a higher level of ritual embodiment, a momentous decision, to be sure. But I did not get the sense that it was the result of a long process of meditation or even deliberation on his part. Michael simply felt that he was strong enough to undergo pamamaku and decided, for matters of convenience, among others, that "I just felt that the time has come to move up my panata." Jackson has no specific set of questions for any of the men. A lot seemed to rest on his instinctive sense of the man standing before him, in his words and comportment, and the intuitive "feel" (tantsya) that one gets from his presence. Once they had proven their sincerity, there was not much by way of further instruction or training. The young men were simply told to refrain from revelry, get a good night's rest, and make sure that they were punctual on the day of the ritual.

The large concrete house close to the crucifixion site had been made into waiting area for the namamaku, where they could dress, pray, and reflect in relative privacy before their ritual. The house also served as a makeshift medical facility, with an assortment of antibiotics, antiseptics, injections, and medical gauze lined up on a table manned by staff whose dress suggested that they were qualified (and prepared) to administer them. Jackson is usually among the first to be nailed, which enables him to support his wards (*alaga*), who would be nailed after him. Before he came out of the house, a media unit filmed him in prayer for a few seconds. As the band played—Sinatra's "My Way"—he submitted himself to the team of nailers, all wearing campaign shirts, by casually walking up to the available cross. Jackson's face was one of calm serenity, his eyes not closed but trained downward, seemingly oblivious to the assembled crowd. Dressed in the red cloak he had used in his previous crucifixions, he calmly lay down on the cross on the ground and dutifully spread his arms out wide on the crossbar, palms open. Two sets of nailers tied his arms to the cross at the elbow. One nailer positioned the nail on Jackson's palm, paused and gestured, not so much as a warning to Jackson but as a prompt to the other nailer with whom he must strike at the same time. As they hammered through each of his palms—three firm hits in quick succession—Jackson let out a wail that indicated pain. With the nails driven through just enough to touch the wood beneath, and with his feet resting on a wooden block attached near its base, the cross was lifted up by three men. After a few seconds, the men rotate the cross 360 degrees on its axis for the assembled crowd to get a glimpse of Jackson's body on the cross. The harsh afternoon sun bore down on Jackson's face, his eyes closed, lips murmuring a prayer, and by all indications calm, serene, and at peace. The band continued playing its tune.

After about fifteen minutes, the cross was brought down by a group of men and once again laid on the ground, where the nailers, again simultaneously, removed the nails from Jackson's palms. Jackson let out a moan, louder than the earlier one, as droplets of blood oozed out of the wound. Isopropyl alcohol was immediately splashed onto his palms as a disinfecting agent, and pieces of cotton and gauze were taped to the wounds to keep the blood from gushing further. Calmly, almost nonchalantly, Jackson rose, walked to the house, and quietly crouched down in the corner with a contented expression from yet another year of fulfilling his panata.

Lucy Reyes

Many people are often surprised when they find out that women are also nailed to the cross on Good Friday. What is the nature of this surprised reaction? The fact that women are also nailed is startling if one's impression of pamamaku is premised on the notion that the ritual is a matter of literalism or imitation oriented toward theatrical authenticity. The surprise is not so much that women have the intestinal fortitude to voluntarily undergo self-mortification. Rather, it lies in the idea that a physical resemblance with Jesus is not a prerequisite for conducting Passion rituals. The presence of female namamaku presents an immediate challenge to the masculinist associations that are often associated with Passion rituals.

In 2011, I met Lucy Reyes at her home in the town of Paombong, in the province of Bulacan, forty kilometers southwest of San Fernando. At fifty-two years of age, Lucy had the reputation of being one of the most famous and influential namamaku in central Luzon. Lucy is identified, in both scholarly and popular accounts, as the principal exemplar for those who embody a fundamental connection between pamamaku and the enhancement of healing capacities (see, for example, Shaw 1992). People from all over the country would visit her to receive the Grace of the Christ-child, the Santo Niño de Pandacan, who channels his healing power through her body. This capacity to be, as she calls it, the "healing instrument" of God did not arise out of any special training or knowledge. It emerges, rather, from nearly two decades of devoting herself to nailing on the cross after being ordered to do so by the Santo Niño himself.

During our meetings, Lucy spoke of seeing Jesus Christ while enduring a particularly severe bout of illness in 1976. She was then eighteen and in the throes of despair, Christ appeared to her as the Santo Niño riding a red bicycle. The Santo Niño did not only cure her but also gave her the capacity and the mandate to heal others. This healing power, however, was not at its peak following that incident. In the ensuing months and years, Christ continued to appear in her dreams and at waking moments, sometimes as the Santo Niño, at others as the Black Nazarene. Each time, Jesus would ask her to perform crucifixion in the manner that was, by the late 1970s, already being conducted in the towns of Pampanga.

Unlike Jackson and Ruben, however, Lucy's participation in pamamaku was in some respects involuntary. Indeed, one of the characteristic features that distinguish the motivations for nailing among women is the direct intervention of God. She describes it as being "taken" by God, which she had initially submitted because she was in an extremely weakened state at that time. The nailing itself was completely directed by the Holy Spirit, who gave specific instructions to her nailers, from the second that the first nail was to be driven to the amount of time she spent on the cross to the prayers that were recited while she was nailed. Dutifully, though not always enthusiastically, Lucy conducted pamamaku for fifteen consecutive years, up to 1992, after which she was nailed at least five more times intermittently. She had stopped the ritual after roughly twenty years upon the explicit and direct instructions of the Santo Niño, who told her, simply, "That's enough."

The documentary film *Nailed* (Shaw 1992) captures Lucy's 1988 pamamaku. The film depicts in gruesome detail how Lucy was made to lie face-down on the Church grounds as two men dressed as centurions whipped and walloped her backside. Later, the film shows the nails going through

Lucy's palms and feet, while a chorus of old women chant the *pasyon* and pray the Our Father. Lucy's countenance is calm and serene. She is shown reciting a speech in the course of her pamamaku:

> For the past thirteen years, I have been one with God. I am part of him today. Look up to me, for I have given you what you have been asking him. My children, hopefully, you will offer your life to me. I am here to grant you all of your wishes. For the past thirteen years that I have been nailed to the cross, it is only now that I'm doing/saying this. Give yourselves to me. Love each other, unite, be generous. I love you, my children, I'm hungry for your love, I love you, and hopefully you'll also love each other. Good afternoon, my children. I am here with you.

Anthropologist Peter Bräunlein (2009, 900), who has focused on ritual practices in the nearby village of Kapitangan, observed that from the 1980s, "more and more people, mostly females, received the command to be crucified in Kapitagan. . . . All of them were healers; all of them were, in the beginning, followers of Lucy, scrutinizing her healing techniques and the way of her crucifixion . . . all of them claimed to have been really chosen by Santo Niño or the Nazarene. All of them compete with each other for the most authentic performance, spiritual power, for disciples and prestige."

Following from the example of Lucy, other prominent female healers who are practitioners of pamamaku include Amparo Santos, known as "Manang Paring" (b. 1941), from Barangay Tiaong in Guiguinto, who has been nailed at least fifteen times since 1986. Mother Paring had the reputation of being particularly capable of withstanding the pain of crucifixion. While nailed to the cross, she was known to recite speeches, sometimes reading from a blank piece of paper, held up by a companion, on moral and themes such as ethical behavior and God's messages to humanity. More recently, a healer named Percy Valencia is typically identified by local and foreign news media as the main attraction of pamamaku events in Kapitangan. It is to the circumstances of Percy's nailing, an event inspired in form, motivation, and outcome by Lucy's first nailing in 1977, that we shall now turn.

Percy Valencia

The female namamaku of Bulacan Province conduct their Passion rituals on the grounds of the Santo Cristo Church in the town of Kapitangan, twenty-six kilometers southwest of San Fernando. The events unfold in the church's courtyard, where there is an elevated cement stage adjacent to a basketball court. Unlike in San Pedro Cutud, there is no apparatus on which a purpose-built cross is attached for the various people "approved" for nailing. When I went there in 2013, a single church pew, taken from the chapel itself, was placed on the front edge of the stage, against which the several wooden crosses were left.

In 2013, there were four namamaku who were brought up on stage to be nailed at thirty-minute intervals beginning at 10:30 in the morning. One of them was Percy Valencia, a female healer from Paombong, who has herself earned the reputation as the most popular female namamaku. Like Lucy and Manang Paring before her, Percy was "taken" by the Santo Nino to perform pamamaku. Like her predecessors, she will continue to do so until she is told to stop by God.

After embarking on a walk of a few hundred along the Kapitangan-Longos Road to the churchyard, Percy was forced to lie face down on the ground while two men took turns whipping and spanking her on the back and buttocks. She was then literally kicked on her backside so that she stumbled forward into a prostrate position, face down on the hot pavement. In this position, the centurions took turns whipping her again with as much force as they could muster, seeming to revel in so doing. One of the men I spoke to later, a man named Jose, told me that it was an important part of the ritual to make it seem that they took pleasure in their beating. After all, he said, the physical humiliation (*kahihiyahan*) of Jesus was part of the Passion.

When Percy arrived in the vicinity of the crucifixion site, her path was cleared by volunteer marshals who whistled the scores of onlookers away. Percy and her group were preceded by three elderly women, who were seemingly lethargic and consumed with emotion as they were led up onto the concrete stage. The women proceeded to chant the *pasyon* as Percy herself was brought on stage and made to lie, arms spread out, on the cross.

Percy herself applied isopropyl alcohol to her palms from a bucket lifted onto her, while the nailers helped saturate and disinfect her feet. When the cross was securely fastened, a man named Tatang Edong began the countdown from three for the first nail to be struck. Two nailers, each with a hammer and nail, then proceeded to nail each of her palms simultaneously. Percy let out a wail of pain as the nails were driven into her palms and feet. After a few minutes, seemingly overcome by the pain and fatigue, she moved between consciousness and unconsciousness. In this state, Percy remained on the cross for about ten minutes, just enough time for the singing of the Lord's Prayer in Tagalog, led by Tatang Edong. It is also at this point that the blood that flowed from the wounds on Percy's feet was collected by her devotees, who believed it to have medicinal properties.

After about twenty minutes on the cross, the centurions unhinged Percy and she was brought immediately into the chapel, still seemingly unconscious. Inside, Percy was laid on the floor in front of the main altar, cradled by an elderly woman who cleaned her wounds as she was fanned and offered drinks to revive her from her ordeal. When she regained semiconsciousness, Percy was taken to a car waiting at the front of the church and driven home.

The facilitative contexts that frame the nailings of Jackson, Lucy and Percy are of a much lower scale than that of Ruben. That is not to say, however, that their pamamaku rituals are less solemn or less meaningful than the more "official" version in San Fernando. Jackson, Lucy, and Percy conduct nailing in response to deeply personal, interiorized sentiments that resonate a subsequent desire to cultivate vertical relationships with the divine. These desires take on particular urgency in the temporal context of Holy Week, during which embodied ritual actions are considered the only adequate means of expressing and manifesting them. Like the interiorized sentiments of utang na loob and tiuala that underscore Ruben's panata, the ritual agencies of non–Via Crucis namamaku are likewise "investments" in that they are premised, at least in part, on the hope that God would respond favorably to painful ritual acts with immanent, in-this-life benefit. This final section had served to show that these investments are in turn mediated by the very diverse life circumstances of each ritual protagonist—whether it is falling from a building, the illness of a loved one, or an apparition from the divine. At this juncture, I would not seek to domesticate this diversity by subjecting them comparative analysis. It would be more fruitful, rather, to examine the broader institutional and ideological contexts in which ritual piety is framed, starting with the Philippine Roman Catholic Church as a formal organization to which each of the namamaku steadfastly claims membership. It is to the theme of "institutions," therefore, that we shall now turn.

PART III

Institutions

Clerical Perspectives on Passion Rituals

In 2004, the Archbishop of Manila, Gaudencio Rosales, issued a four-page pastoral message urging his congregation to watch Mel Gibson's film *The Passion of the Christ*. In its vivid portrayal of the crucifixion and death of Christ, *Time* magazine ranked it first among the "ten most ridiculously violent movies" of the past few decades (Sanburn 2010). In spite of its depiction of "crimson carnage," the archbishop encouraged his flock to encounter Jesus through this movie, emphasizing that "a great number of leaders of Christian churches have hailed the film as a credible, effective and superb cinematic narration of the Gospel story." Watching it was, in fact, nothing short of an expression of moral virtue: "A genuine Lenten good deed . . . this encounter with Jesus will itself be an encounter with his grace." The archbishop recommended that viewers "try to enter deeply into the last hours of Jesus and let those final hours work their way into your mind and heart" (Rosales 2004).

Five years later, the subject of profoundly experiencing the suffering of Christ in the "minds and hearts" of Filipinos was again a topic addressed by the now Cardinal Rosales. In 2009, the cardinal commented on the actions of devotees to the Black Nazarene, or suffering Christ, who are traditionally known to be among the most passionate and vehement in their ritual behavior: "Actually, [the devotees] are the fanatics. That's exactly the devotion we want to purify. Sometimes, the strong emotion of people takes over reason. The emotions take over the holiness of [Holy Week], the emotions take over the devotion. The emotions, the fanaticism, they should not be there and that is exactly what we are trying to tell the people. We still have a long way to go" (Macarain 2009). The cardinal's statement posits "strong emotions" as a corollary of "holiness." A piety driven by the former may lead to strong religious fervor, but one that has a corrosive effect that tarnishes the faith as a whole. The religious fanatic is consumed by gut feelings, sentimentality, and intuitive sensation, and is overly consumed with the kinds of misdirected enthusiasm that leads to "impure" modes of piety. Clerics have "a long way to go" in addressing these issues because their voices of reason are drowned out by the very fanaticism that they seek to "purify."

The two instances above demonstrate the spectrum of the Filipino response to the suffering Christ, which can range from viewing the imagery of extreme corporeal violence as "a genuine Lenten good deed" to an illicit and impure mode of piety driven by "strong emotion of people [that] takes over reason." The cardinal's statements highlight the importance of coming to a more nuanced understanding of the clerical point of view of how Filipino Catholics should relate to the suffering of Christ, particularly when it involves ritual actions that may be construed as extreme or driven by profound sentimentality, as we have seen with Passion rituals such as pabasa, pagdarame, and pamamaku king krus.

In this chapter, I address the nature and diversity of clerical responses to the Filipino ritual investment in the suffering Christ. One the one hand, there are those attitudes of condemnation that dismiss vehement ritual actions as "wrong" or "illicit" and even "fanatic" versions of proper piety. It is indeed important to discuss what the Church's official position on Passion rituals is and why this is held, both from the perspective of the clergy themselves and according to how they are officially conveyed in official church edicts and promulgations. What is it, exactly, that makes Passion rituals problematic from a theological and doctrinal point of view?

On the other hand, it must not be underestimated that there are many instances of clerical accommodation and tolerance of Passion rituals, which stem from a certain level of sympathy for the sentimental intent of ritual agents. Looking at individual actions and perspectives, it is the case that the clerics "on the ground" engage with ritual practitioners in a much more varied and nuanced way than what can be inferred from the Church's official proclamations. How can we make sense of the multifaceted nature of clerical responses to Passion rituals? How can we reconcile the attitudes of condemnation that dismiss Passion rituals as "wrong," "illicit," and even "fanatic" with those others that see them as manifestations of a visceral piety?

My response to this problematic is framed by my engagement with several clerics in central Luzon and beyond, but particularly with Pampanga's highest-ranking cleric, His Excellency Archbishop Paciano Aniceto (more popularly known as "Apo Ceto"), at the Mother of Good Counsel Seminary where he resides. One cannot easily overestimate Apo Ceto's popularity, not only as one of the most experienced and highly respected prelates in the Philippines, but also as a true son of the province who has the adoration and affection of anyone who would consider themselves a proud Kapampangan Catholic. My encounter with Apo Ceto gave me a firsthand impression of the complexity of clerical opinion, particularly as it pertains to the practice of Passion rituals in Pampanga. But it also gave me a framework in which to contextualize this complexity in a way that sheds some light into how Passion rituals are construed from an "official" perspective.

My main contention is that the diversity of clerical perspectives on Passion rituals are not contradictions per se but are discursive facets of the critical encounter between gospel and culture. As such, I align the spectrum of clerical responses within the discourse of "inculturation," which we discuss here in a more expansive sense as an attitude and ethical framework rather than simply as an official doctrine of the Roman Catholic Church. By considering how inculturation has pervaded clerical discourse over the past four decades, we have a rubric with which to frame both sides of the spectrum. How does an institution like the Roman Catholic Church intervene in notions of personhood?

Clerical Denouncement

In April 2012, I received a phone call from Allan Navarro, the director of the Via Crucis, an event that features the most publicized nailing ritual in the Philippines. He asked whether I would be interested in appearing on a show broadcast on the local TV station called *So To Speak*. Apo Ceto, he told me, would be one of the guests, along with the Via Crucis "Kristo," Ruben Enaje, as well as the head of the San Fernando tourism board. The choice of the panelists was telling. Allan and Ruben would ostensibly represent the perspective of the Passion ritual practitioners throughout the province; Apo Ceto, who was well known to hold views that frowned upon the continued practice of Passion rituals, would represent the Church view, which was commonly assumed to be against the practice of these rituals.

I declined the invitation but watched the program with great interest. Allan and Ruben, on cue, expressed their views that they had narrated many times before—of *panata*, *darame*, and the life stories that contextualized it. The Apo Ceto who responded, however, was of a different persona than the one I had spoken with two years before. He was forceful in labeling Passion rituals as an "external display" that would dissuade even him from wanting to be a Catholic if this meant having to have himself nailed to the cross. Are these rituals a sin? he was asked. "It is a caricature of the real meaning of religion," said the archbishop, before quoting Saint Paul: "The body is the temple of God, and if you violate this temple, God will punish you."

If one reads newspapers and listen to the news during Holy Week in the Philippines, one is likely to find a priest or cleric like Apo Ceto, who, at least in public, "discourages," "frowns upon," or "disapproves of" Passion rituals. Many of these opinions come from the highest levels of the Church hierarchy. Yet rather than condemn "fanatics" as beyond salvation, critical responses such as these serve to emphasize the continuing mandate of the Church and its leaders in guiding ritual practitioners on how to reorient their practice in the right direction. This reorientation begins with an elaboration on why these rituals are problematic from a doctrinal and theological point of view.

The first and most commonly cited criticism is that participation in Passion rituals affects the frequency of Church-sanctioned sacramental participation. In 2008, for example, a prominent monsignor speaking on behalf of the Catholic Bishops Conference of the Philippines (CBCP) explicitly associated the practices of darame and pamamaku as manifestations of superstition and inauthentic faith, even if the practitioner declares faith in Christ and in Catholicism: "We are doubtful if these activities outside the parishes are real expressions of the Christian faith. We believe these are expressions of superstitious belief and usually done out of a need for money and tourism purposes" (Punay 2008). In placing the practice "outside the parish," the monsignor is reiterating the distant provincial occurrence of the practice, and making explicit associations with moral bankruptcy motivated by an opportunistic desire for profit and notoriety, not faith. In a 2013 address to the Church-run Radio Veritas, a Cebu archbishop who was then president of the CBCP stated that more emphasis must be placed on the Church-sanctioned and prescribed ways of commemorating the occasion of Christ's Passion: "We know that we have been practicing this in principle for a long time[, but] I hope that we could emphasize more the spirit of prayer. . . . Beginning Holy Thursday with the washing of the feet and the Visita Iglesia, these are two wonderful ways of celebrating Holy Week" (Tubeza 2013). In essence, a few of the clerics I spoke with identified this as a problem of sacerdotalism. While the self-flagellants may engage more corporeally with Christ's Passion, the absence of the consecrating power of the priest renders the physical engagement with Christ's Passion impotent and, in the end, illegitimate. Apo Ceto reiterated this position when I spoke with him in 2010. He was adamant in his conviction that only the sacraments offered the true way of taking up Christ's invitation, and that everyone should be one with Christ by participating "fully and properly" in the community of the official Church.

Another critical theme in the clerical perceptions of Passion rituals concerns the fundamental misunderstanding and underappreciation of the nature Christ's message of salvation. In more specific terms, Passion rituals that have a strong focus on Christ's crucifixion are thought to be unappreciative of the full significance of the Paschal mystery, which stresses the bipartite nature of Christian salvation involving Christ's death and his resurrection. In one sense, as Apo Ceto stressed during his *So To Speak* interview, Holy Week "does not end on Good Friday," pointing to the underestimation of the importance of Easter Sunday. The archbishop is here referring to the notion that the fixation on pain in the course of flagellation imbues Good Friday with a sense of climax that relegates the resurrection event to "second billing." The archbishop had acknowledged that Filipinos have a cultural tendency toward relating to the "drama" of suffering.

This tendency has been officially addressed by the Philippine Roman Catholic Church. In its "Pastoral Letter on Filipino Spirituality," rituals of pamamaku are characterized as being mistakenly premised on the notion that Holy Week terminates on Good Friday, as though completely ignoring the event of the Resurrection. The Letter draws upon the scriptures to correct such a misimpression: "Our faith does not ever encourage a morbid embrace of pain, suffering and death as apart from the victorious liberation achieved by our Lord Jesus Christ. The Gospel has never extolled suffering as separate from the edification symbolized by the Kingdom of God, as we find in Matthew 5:1-12; 13:44)" (CBCP 1999)

The sentiment of underestimating the soteriological importance of the Resurrection is a sentiment that has been echoed by the Philippine's national artist for literature, Nick Joaquin, who observed, "It's clear that the Filipino feels more drawn to Christ the Suffering Victim than to Christ the Risen Victor." Of all the reasons put fourth to explain this, Joaquin argues that "the correct explanation is, quite simply, history," and in that vein situates the arrival of Christianity in the Philippines during a period of Christ's humanization during which "Maundy Thursday and Good Friday became in themselves great and autonomous feats" (Joaquin 1987, 1).

Referring to the continuance of self-flagellation in spite of Church criticism of the practice, an article by Navarro titled "Lenten Madness" in Manila's *Malaya Newspaper* declares, "Other countries have long gone around this inevitable disparagement of Lent as a dreary religious obligation. . . . Understandably, the Western world, particularly the Americans, have come to focus their Holy Week celebrations not the on dark and forbidding message of Maundy Thursday and Good Friday, but on the unalloyed joy of Easter Sunday." This stands in stark contrast to "cults" of self-flagellants in Pampanga, who are doing nothing but demonstrating "the Filipinos' morbid obsession with death and damnation . . . that owes its awesome power to the compelling logic of blind and unquestioning obedience" (Navarro 1991, 6).

In another sense, there is a belief that Passion rituals manifest a redundant understanding of the salvific meaning of the Paschal mystery. "If you truly believe that Christ has already suffered for you," says Father Martin, a parish priest in Manila with whom I had a conversation in 2012, "then you must realize that physically taking on his pain is like disregarding his act of sacrifice—like saying that it wasn't enough. The sacrifice of Jesus does not need to be repeated." Father Martin points to the book of Hebrews, which describes Jesus' "perfect Sacrifice" that is eternal and sufficient to expiate all human sin, not just specific sins of those in his generation or of specific individuals. Finally, he emphasized that it is somewhat "arrogant" to think that one's physical sacrifice could ever match the significance of Jesus' pain. "No amount of pain can be enough to wash away your sins," he insisted, "especially not without any form of penance or attending church."

The lamentation of doctrinal redundancy expressed by Father Martin is a theme that has been expressed in the public media for at least the last four decades. A 1977 article titled "Lent's Delirium" conveys the tone of such laments in its questioning of the necessity of flagellation, given that Christ had already redeemed the sins of man in his crucifixion. "It is as though Christ stayed nailed on the cross and was never heard from again. Christ on the cross is a synthesis of man's suffering. For indeed man's way is the way of the cross. In all other days of our lives, you and I don't want for crosses to bear. Of that, we have plenty. So who needs to look for crosses?" (Magsanoc 1977, 5). Letty Magsanoc expresses a discourse of lamentation that effectively demarcates and limits proper, reasonable, and logical Catholicism from its extreme, fanatic, and "delirious" rendition.

The redundancy of corporal self-flagellation would seem to be challenged by scriptural verses that extol the virtues of "imitating Christ," for us to "take up one's cross and follow him" (Mark 8:34). When it was put to him by the interviewer that Pope John Paul II himself engaged in flagellation in the tradition of other saintly exemplars, Apo Ceto admitted that this was in line with Biblical teaching, but pointed out that this must be private, and it is normally reserved for monks (and even for them, it is optional, "not because they are punishing or hating, but because they are showing self-mastery over the body, allowing themselves to show closer union with God. It is not just gratuitous pain or punishment; it's a form of prayer."). Father Martin echoed this sentiment: "Do they know that Jesus will return? That he will come back, at the day of Judgment, and no matter how many times you whip yourself, it won't save you unless you are truly righteous?"

Clerical Accommodation

In spite of his critical public stance, I was very intrigued by Apo Ceto's expression of tolerance for and even admiration of the cultural aspect of Passion rituals. In our interview in 2010, he expressed a somewhat softer and more accommodating perspective on those who self-flagellate, drawing from his own recollection of having grown up in Pampanga: "Actually, [self-flagellation] is practiced in San Fernando because it is our tradition. I have been around [flagellants] ever since I was young, and they have been around since before anyone can remember. One time, I remember being approached by a [flagellant] who told me that he would sacrifice so that his sick mother would get well. He acted in good faith and was offering something to God, and I could see that his prayers were so strong and fervent."

It is not uncommon for clerics to express a sense of sympathy for those who continue to conduct the ritual as a matter of cultural expression. While Apo Ceto expresses this view in private, others have indeed gone "on record" with these sentiments and even do things that suggest at least tacit encouragement for the continuance of the practice. In a program aired in 2002 on the National Geographic Channel, for example, a priest in Pampanga points to a religiosity among self-mortifiers in Pampanga that is commendable for continually pushing the boundaries of piety toward a deeper commitment to the promises of salvation: "The Filipino has a very deep sense of suffering. And crucifixion, flagellation and other forms of self-inflicted pain during Holy week is, I think, an expression of the Filipino's measuring himself, how far he could go" (Abraham 2002).

Similarly, in a blog called *The Faith of a Centurion* (and in an article titled "The Flagellants and 'Kristos' of Lent: Simple Folks Keep the Faith"), a Jesuit priest expresses what he says is a common opinion among clerics, who laud the motivation of self-mortifiers even though they question the manner in which it is expressed: "I find the extent and intensity of these [self-flagellants] fervor laudable and personally humbling. Compared to them, I may indeed be a lesser Christian. If I can't do what they do on Good Friday or on any Fridays in the season of Lent, then there is more to it than what I see" (Gonzalez 2010).

It is fairly common to observe priests act upon their sympathy for the motivations of self-mortifiers by directly engaging with them in the course of their ritual practice. It is crucial to note that such lines of encouragement do not constitute a contravention of Church policies, mainly because expressions and actions of admiration and sympathy are always tempered by a reiteration of the importance of sacramental and doctrinal participation as a supplement, if not corrective, to these ritual practices.

I learned a great deal about Church policy from my discussions with a bishop in Angeles City, who, in addition to being an environmental activist, is arguably the most recognizable scholar-prelate in the province as the cohost of a weekly television program aimed at helping the laity make sense of the scriptures. He is also recognized as someone who openly interacted with the flagellants, which was as, Robert Tantingco (2012) described it, "his subtle way of weaning them away from the folk Bible to the real Bible." One of the most important things the bishop reiterated was that theological issues must be contextualized according to the cultural and sociopolitical realities of Filipino Catholics in Pampanga. He encouraged a deep appreciation for the distinctive features of "Kapampangan culture," and was always open to considering culturalist explanations as equally applicable in understanding the rationale of Passion rituals. The bishop was adamant that the persistence of self-flagellation was a sign of their continuing mandate as cleric-healers whose responsibility is met through the enactment of a spiritual treatment regime. In the end, however, he was of the opinion that the cultural factors that condition how scriptures are disseminated and received are crucial, and for a true appreciation of this we need to think about a broader spectrum of clerical insights, particularly from priests on the ground.

Other priests I've spoken to in towns in Santa Ana and Bacolor have also allowed self-mortifiers to use church premises, and even admitted to blessing the whips and the crosses used for flagellation. One pastoral custodian from Pampanga's Mamacalulu shrine welcomed self-flagellants onto the church premises, where he blessed and prayed over them, and sang the Biblical passage "Whosoever wants to be my disciple, go and take up your cross and follow me." This was motivated by his deep sense of respect for self-mortifiers; the custodian declared, "I've not seen Catholics pray as intensely as that flagellant prayed." Following the example of the bishop from Angeles, the custodian made the self-flagellants promise that they would attend church after their ritual, and preferably visit the confessional booth. These acts of consecrating Passion rituals, therefore, were in a sense a conditional delegation of responsibility to self-flagellants, who may be allowed to perform their rituals so long as they make a conscious effort to imbue their practice with church-prescribed modes of piety.

Inculturation and Passion Rituals

It would not be accurate to reduce the Church's position to a blindly critical stance. Indeed, as the second part of the chapter has demonstrated, there is a diversity of public and clerical opinion on Passion rituals, some of which emphasize the Church institution's inclusionary rather than exclusionary mandate. This is not to say that clerics who show tacit approval of Passion rituals are acting against Church directives. In many of these more positive attitudes towards Passion rituals, individual clerics are in fact drawing from an officially sanctioned theological framework of "inculturation." A way to make sense of the diversity of clerical declarations, therefore, lies in an appreciation of the relevance of this concept to the Philippine religious landscape, and in particular, the practical and conceptual elasticity inherent in its implementation.

Inculturation is a concept and an attitude that places primacy in fostering a mutual interaction between gospel and the culture of those who are the subject of evangelizing work. It is, at its core, a recognition that culture is a locus of divine revelation. As it is described in the Federation of Asian Bishop's Conference (FABC Theological Advisory Commission 1991), "Inculturation consists not only in the expression of the Gospel and the Christian faith through the cultural medium, but includes, as well, experiencing, understanding and appropriating the Gospel through the cultural resources of a people" (see also Fabella 2004, 119). While inculturation calls for the Gospel to be adapted to culture, the latter is simultaneously seen as a target to be evaluated, realigned, and changed. Documents from the Second Vatican Council define "inculturation" as an encounter that "entails transformation of the authentic values of these cultures by their integration into Christianity" (Flannery 1984, 813). The theological scholar Virginia Fabella (1999, 126) observes that while inculturation identifies culture as the means by which the good news is made meaningful, "culture must also take the Gospel seriously. It must allow itself to be critiqued, purified and transformed by the gospel." In the critical encounter between Gospel and culture, the latter is conceived as both the medium of revelation and the subject of reorientation.

On the one hand, a critical view of Passion rituals is consistent with the principles of inculturation. To express views that disavow the superfluity and redundancy of these practices, along with the critique that they have a negative effect upon the practitioner's sacramental participation, can be seen as a deployment of the reorientative mandate of inculturation. In their Pastoral Exhortation on Philippine Culture (O. Cruz 1999), conveyed by then CBCP president Oscar Cruz, the Catholic Bishops Conference of the Philippines calls for the kind of inculturation that applies a critical attentiveness to the "inhumanity and hardness of heart present in all human cultures and individuals." To the extent that Passion Rituals manifest a redundant and incomplete appreciation of the Paschal mystery, declarations of "fanaticism" or "illicitness" channel the critical attentiveness and discernment implied in inculturation about what is "contra human" and "contra Gospel" within the culture. The critical attentiveness to the cultural disposition toward what is "contra human" is commensurate with the main goal of inculturation, which is to reorient local culture toward a complete and profound understanding of the Paschal mystery. Inculturation calls for the good news of the Gospel to be "incarnated" in every local culture with which it comes into contact—a condition that prevails when people are made to understand that upon his resurrection, Jesus had effectively transcended the confines of local particularity. As José De Mesa (1979, 21) puts it, the soteriological message of inculturation is that Jesus "must be born, die and live anew in every culture, history and people for these to be purified, perfected and ennobled."

The more tolerant and accommodating attitudes and actions toward Passion rituals also find resonance within the framework of inculturation. This resonance is based primarily on how inculturation presupposes a particular a "postmodern" notion of a culture that continues to manifest the influence of precolonial beliefs and tendencies. The primary example of the "diversity" of culture is "popular religiosity," which occurs because "even after centuries of evangelization, the common folk retained their pre-Christian beliefs and practices while professing the Christian faith, unaware of the inconsistencies between the two religious systems" (Fabella 1999, 124).

In the Pastoral Exhortation on Philippine Culture, Filipino cultural tradition is characterized as possessing several discernible characteristics that can be summarized as family, authority, and divinity. While the exhortation acknowledges the primacy of family in a unified Filipino culture, the Church believes it to be mediated by a predilection for vertical power relations, "those elements that have to do with authority and hierarchy." Filipino culture is also predisposed to personalism, which places primacy on the values of hospitality and reciprocity. Filipino culture is "dependent on the benevolence of a transcendent being." It is this dependence that guides action in moments of struggle: "Our religiosity provides a moral anchor to individuals when confronted with a personal crisis." (O. Cruz 1999).

A more accommodating approach to Passion rituals is premised upon a view of culture as having two facets. First, culture is not a static, immutable set of mores and beliefs that do not change over time. The dynamism of culture is such that it is constantly being shaped by different influences. In this sense, cultural tradition is not so much an inheritance of practices and beliefs preserved in its authentic state as a historically contingent process of adaptation to foreign influence (whether imposed or otherwise). The Second Plenary Council of the Philippines took inspiration from the Second Vatican Council's emphasis on a more modernist concept of culture, which acknowledges and even celebrates the diversity within it. "Ours is a pluralist society and a prime factor of our pluralism is the diversity of our cultural heritage. Lowland cultures have been heavily influenced by three centuries of Spanish colonial rule, the Muslim people of the south by Islamic traditions, and the mountain tribes, especially on Luzon, Mindanao and Mindoro, have retained much of their pre-Spanish characteristics" (O. Cruz 1999).

Second, the Church's accommodating stance on Passion rituals is framed on an understanding of culture as, primarily, a repository of values. In the Pastoral Statement on Philippine Culture, this is stated explicitly: "Values, thus, are at the deepest level of culture—they are its heart and core. They are, for all intents and purposes, what give people their identity as a people, a distinct human society" (O. Cruz 1999). The dynamics of culture lies in the possibility of redefining and reorienting even long-held traditional values, of changing institutionalized and ingrained traits and characteristics.

Incultured Passion

Roman Catholic clerics in the Philippines are very attentive to the ritual practices of their flocks, and are explicit in the extent to which they resonate with official church teaching. The tone and content of prevalent media depictions of Passion rituals, however, reinforce the tendency to reduce the institutional Church's attitudes and response to a caricature of its official proclamations. From an exclusively discursive perspective, one gets the impression that Roman Catholic clerics in the Philippines are strict and uncompromising in enforcing the doctrinal prohibition against rituals of self-mortification. While it is indeed important to inquire into the Church's official position regarding Passion rituals, as we have done in the first part of this essay, it is also important to consider that there are attitudes and actions of tolerance and flexibility that infuse the actual, "on-the-ground" deployment of evangelical responsibilities.

It is in the spirit of accounting for the diversity and even contradiction of clerical discourse that this chapter has been conceptualized. This has entailed a discussion of the conceptual paradigms by which the Church in the Philippines understands the nature of culture and of personhood itself. This has given a more nuanced perspective on the seeming contradiction between the critical or more accommodating attitudes toward ritual agencies that fall outside the scope of doctrinal or sacramental adherence. I have argued that a consideration of the conceptual elasticity of inculturation is a way of being more attuned to how the seeming contradiction in perspectives on the rituals can be accounted for on a theological level.

The Roman Catholic Church has never been content to limit its involvement in the lives of Filipinos to theology. Although the agents of the Church premise their attitudes and actions toward ritual agency on their interpretations of official proscriptions, the Church as an institution has also been active in contextualizing Filipino realities beyond the ritual sphere. It is to how the Church acts with other institutional forces to reinscribe the meaning of "suffering selfhood" that we shall turn in the next chapter.

Suffering Selfhood in Transnational Domains

In April 1988, the then Philippine president Corazon Aquino stood before overseas Filipino workers (OFWs) in Hong Kong's Saint Margaret's Church to acknowledge the enormous economic and social benefits of their "suffering." "It is not only your relatives who are grateful for your sacrifices," she said, "but also the entire nation." (Republic of the Philippines Presidential Management Staff (PMS). 1992; see also Franco 2011). For indeed OFWs were not merely overseas workers who remit huge sums of foreign capital back to the Philippines. She called them *bagong bayani*— "modern-day heroes"—who are ensuring the very survival of the Philippine nation. It mattered greatly that the OFWs were hearing the speech from Cory Aquino, for she herself had suffered through the death of her once-exiled husband, Ninoy, at the hands of an excessive dictatorial regime. Ninoy has been immortalized by his martyric declaration, "The Filipino is worth dying for." After all, as historians Vicente Rafael (2000) and Reynaldo Ileto (1998) have argued, the concept of heroism in the Philippines is not simply premised on a notion of organic patriotism per se but is instead built upon the example of a pantheon of nationalist-martyrs such as José Rizal and Ninoy, whose lives, as Rafael (2000, 211) put it, "merge into a single narrative frame that harked back to the themes of the [Passion of Christ] . . . of innocent lives forced to undergo humiliation at the hands of alien forces."

It was only fitting, therefore, that that the speech was delivered in a church, which is not just a place of worship for many OFWs but a place where they can find solace and material support, if not directly from Church-aligned advocacy groups then from informal support networks. The venue served to emphasize that Roman Catholic institutions have played a very crucial role in legitimizing the discursive force of the nation state's ethos by infusing the ideal of modern-day heroism with notions of Christlike martyrdom. The Catholic Bishops' Conference of the Philippines (CBCP) has a fairly long track record in this regard. Even just a few weeks before Corazon Aquino's bagong bayani speech, the then-president of the CBCP, archbishop Leonardo Legaspi (1988), associated the suffering of OFWs with divine reward in stating, "For every pain, there is also joy. For every sacrifice, there is a corresponding good. Migration of peoples, in whatever form or for whatever reason, has always foreshadowed the unfolding of greater designs of God." In this way, the Church institution has been complicit in cultivating the salience of an idealized national discourse in which confronting the necessary demands and contingencies of global capital—the tumultuous terrain in which bagong bayani risk their lives and suffer for the nation—is depicted as coterminous with the soteriological ideal of Christian salvation.

In this chapter, I examine how the notion of suffering selfhood that forms the conceptual backbone of this book finds resonance in domains outside of the ritual spaces in which it is conducted. How have formal institutions, both religious and state, promulgated particular ideas of suffering through the evocation of Christ's example? I discuss how the Roman Catholic Church is complicit in physically and discursively encouraging OFWs to craft themselves into ethical agents of the most pious and most esteemed kind.[1] Echoing the processes that anthropologists Valentina Napolitano and Kristin Norget (2009) have described as occurring within "economies of sanctity," I consider how the institution of the Filipino Roman Catholic Church positions OFW labor within a global, exemplary Catholic imaginary, one promulgated by formal declarations that publicly valorize OFWs as virtuously suffering, de facto missionaries. As the example of Corazon Aquino above suggests, I argue that it is not the Church institution alone that accomplishes this. In the second part of the chapter, I discuss how the idea of "export quality martyrs" undergirds the state bureaucracy's ability to promulgate a national discourse of exemplary suffering and new heroism as a way to legitimize its neoliberal pursuit of foreign capital. This discourse finds resonance, too, in the way ritual agency—even those channeled in the three Passion rituals I discuss in this book—is thought to be commensurate with one's participation in the global economy.

The OFW as Suffering Hero Missionaries

The role of the Church in supporting OFWs is recognized by Filipino clerics as an important part of their pastoral responsibilities. Take, for example, the perspectives of Father Martin, a Roman Catholic parish priest from Manila, with whom I spoke about the concept of suffering in transnational domains. While he expressed interest in discussing the nature of the OFW economy, our conversation often shifted to official church views on the corrosive effect of wealth on the moral and spiritual lives of OFWs. Father Martin narrated some scenarios in which OFW families had disintegrated as a result of migrant workers succumbing to the allure of financial empowerment. "Why did [he] buy all that iPhone and things for himself . . . are you not going to put [the money] to your children? Why not save the money, or at least put it to a *sari-sari* [provision] store?" These were rhetorical questions not meant to encourage OFWs to commit to monastic self-denial. Rather, Father Martin's views pointed to an idea of martyric virtue no longer premised on the necessity of death but rather on the very act of struggle and perseverance in the tumultuous transnational domain. "The bagong bayani," he clarified, "it is about sweat."

Father Martin's sentiments resonate with the larger institutional Philippine Catholic Church position. Unlike the strong rationalist orientation of the state in promoting foreign labor, official Church pronouncements extoll the virtues of persevering through the hardships of overseas deployment, characterizing it as a sacrifice that will eventually be repaid with not only economic but also deferred spiritual reward. As religious studies scholar Robert Ellwood (1988, 137) put it, "The idea that poverty could be a state of blessedness in itself, a favorite of preachers as recently as a century ago, is now hopelessly discredited . . . even the most conservative puppeteers nowadays exhort their poor to get ahead, but to do it by nonviolent means."

The Church's material investment in OFW pastoral care is consistent with its mandate as it was promulgated in the Second Vatican Council in 1963–1965, and more specifically in the Second Plenary Council of the CBCP (PCP-II) in 1991. In these gatherings, clerics reiterated the Church's responsibility to develop the total human person, which referred not just to matters of mysticism or spirituality but also to the Church's role in cultivating economic self-reliance among its flock.[2] The Church's role in the preservation and enhancement of OFW labor power is itself an expression of specific forms of religious governmentality. In describing "economies of sanctity," Napolitano and Norget (2009, 253) refer to how Roman Catholic institutions actively promote processes of "recirculation, mimesis and re-localization" to foster an "embodied sense of belonging and allegiance to a larger, global Catholic community and project." The Filipino Catholic Church's endorsement of suffering is undergirded by the affirmation of OFW suffering and the valorization of OFWs as martyrs by way of effort, rather than of death, as well as by the identification of transnational domains as the terrain of a new spiritual frontier in the global mission of Roman Catholic expansion.

Overseas Filipino workers are characterized as exemplary individuals who, although suffering in foreign contexts, nevertheless manage to remain "productive." This theme was strongly resonant in CBCP pastoral letters between the late 1980s and mid-1990s. From a Church perspective, this productivity through suffering does not merely refer to workers' economic contributions but also to their roles as de facto missionaries in overseas missionary fields otherwise inaccessible to clerical activity. This notion of exemplary martyrdom echoes what anthropologist Maya Mayblin (2014) described among Roman Catholics in Brazil, who are singled out for public praise and respectful treatment as *sofredors* (sufferers). Mayblin construes such recognition as forms of "consummation," in which "a person's hidden sacrifices are acknowledged and, as such, made productive" (356).

A primary example of this is the 1995 "Pastoral Letter on Filipino Migrant Workers," which endorsed the Migrant Workers and Overseas Filipinos Act. The letter affirmed the relevance of the words of Pope Pius XII, who in 1957 had reiterated the virtue of persevering through hardship: "The phenomenon of the modern emigration undoubtedly follows its own laws, but it is really Divine Wisdom which makes use of human events, including sad ones at times, in order to fulfill the design of salvation for the benefit of the whole of mankind. . . . We are convinced that this is true with regard to Filipino migration." The letter characterized the experience of overseas labor in the logic of sacrifice amid moral and physical danger:

> Our reflection moves us, first of all, to thank the Filipinos abroad for the manifold sacrifices they have undertaken for us here at home. Their endurance in the face of adverse conditions, their determination to turn risks into opportunities, their courage in the face of real physical threats (for example, seamen in the Persian Gulf) and moral dangers are to be admired. The courage of these migrant workers has shown us how to believe in life and to hope against many odds. (Morelos 1995).

The 1995 CBCP letter pointed to the example of "our migrant saint," San Lorenzo Ruiz, the first Filipino martyred while serving in overseas mission. Father Martin echoed the spirit of this mimesis: "We should look to [San Lorenzo], for he was, in a way, an OFW too [in] helping with the Church mission overseas." By drawing an association between OFWs and saintly exemplars such as San Lorenzo, labor migration is effectively identified as a new spiritual frontier in the global mission of Roman Catholic expansion. For OFWs do not simply constitute economic units but also serve as de facto missionaries who, even in the pursuit of economic advancement, contribute to spreading the faith.

The 1991 PCP-II indeed lauded the dispersal of Filipino workers as a solution to the challenges of declining rates of sacramental adherence. Far from emphasizing a prosperity gospel in the conventional sense (Koning 2009; Wiegele 2005; Tremlett 2014), official CBCP pastoral letters, as well as published opinion pieces from well-respected Catholic bishops in the early 2000s, are explicit about the missionary potential of Filipino migrant workers. Three examples can be cited in this regard.

First, in the "Pastoral Letter on the Church's Mission in the New Millennium," archbishop Orlando Quevedo (2000), then the CBCP's president, reiterated this potential with clarity: "Our overseas workers have in so many instances become missionaries, bringing the Gospel and Faith where these have not been present, renewing and reactivating Christian life and practice where these have been in decline." Second, a letter by bishop Precioso Cantillas of Maasin (2005) similarly reiterated the support of the Church for overseas migration, acknowledging that OFWs "not only work for 'more bread' to feed their families; by their witness they also 'feed' the whole world the Bread—the word of God made flesh in Jesus Christ." Third, and most explicit on this theme, is Jesuit father Victor Badillo (2010), who characterized OFWs as "missionaries [although] they have not been missioned . . . [who] fill empty churches, fill the air with joyous Hontiveros songs, praising God. They are the answer to the prayer of parish priests who have only a few old people left in the parish." Badillo depicts the duty of care among OFWs as a not merely a relationship of domestic intimacy but also a platform of evangelical opportunity that would be otherwise inaccessible by conventional forms of missionization. This is particularly so given the religious disaffection that arises from the demands of modern-day life. In this context, "many a fallen-away Catholic returns to the faith of their fathers led by a child catechized by a yaya [maid]. A Filipina, taking care of children left alone by parents keeping up with the Joneses, shares the essentials of the Faith. . . . The OFWs, who stayed away from churches at home, become fervent Catholics and even become apostles. In Christianizing others, they Christianize themselves" (Badillo 2010). These three statements by well-known and respected clerics portray overseas work as a convergence of civic and spiritual responsibilities, reiterating the very concrete link between being a "bagong bayani" and a spiritual crusader for the Church: "Ang bagong bayani ng bayan are also bagong bayani ng simbahan" (The new heroes of the nation are also the new heroes of the Church) (Badillo 2010).

Although no one would explicitly call themselves a "new hero of the church," a survey by Scott Solomon (2009, 294–295) found that 88 percent of the 691 OFWs in Hong Kong either "strongly agreed" (44 percent) or "agree" (44 percent) that indeed they are "heroes" (see also Franco 2011, 58). It is more common among OFWs, however, to hear what they do described as "suffering," "sacrifice," and even "martyrdom" (nagpapaka-martyr). This points to how public affirmation by religious institutions of OFW as suffering martyrs and new missionaries has conditioned and substantiated a particular kind of sentimentality about OFWs in both the public and political domain.

The discursive currency of new heroism of the nation and the Church, propelled largely through a postauthoritarian liberalization of the mass media, evokes culturally resonant themes of pity and empathy (Franco 2011, 137). To feel pity, or awa, is not to think of their situation as a cautionary example of the pitfalls of devoting oneself to the nation but rather as a noble contribution to a higher good. Contemporary school textbooks contain examples of OFWs who have paid the ultimate price in the course of their overseas deployment.[3] The evocation of sentiments of pity and empathic solidarity for such fallen martyr-missionaries reiterated the nobility of their overseas deployment, in spite of the real dangers associated with such work. It is important to note that the logic of suffering and sacrifice has a political and economic component that is emphasized more strongly by state programs and institutions. It is to this that we shall now turn.

Suffering as Export-Quality Martyrs

Sencho Roman is a forty-year-old technician from the Philippine province of Pampanga who, for most of the last fifteen years, has whipped his own back to a bloody pulp in a ritual commemorating Jesus Christ's Passion on Good Friday. When I spoke to him in 2012, he told me that he began self-flagellating on behalf of his mother, Meling, who worked as a domestic helper in Hong Kong to earn enough money to service a family debt. Sencho's flagellation, as a ritual embodiment of the physical sacrifice of Christ, was performed as a means of appealing for God's help in alleviating the family's financial situation. Years after his first whipping, Sencho too would leave Pampanga to take up employment in the Middle East, a transnational sacrifice he took on with a self-confident machismo that extended from the ritual experience. "No problem," he recalled, "If I could flagellate, I knew I could handle Saudi." The capacity for ritual embodiment to bring about masculine potency brings to mind religious studies scholar Paul-François Tremlett's (2006, 15) observations among Filipino men who participate in the Black Nazarene procession in Manila, in which seeking proximity to the image of the suffering Christ offered a means to "transcend a condition of weakness and vulnerability." Yet for all the strength Sencho acquired from flagellation, narrating this had brought back memories of his mother, who had since passed away due to illness. "My flagellation is painful to the body, even though I'm a man. But that's nothing compared to how she sacrificed for us in Hong Kong. She's the [real] hero . . . she's the martyr."

Heads of state since Corazon Aquino have made constant and frequent references to the "suffering" and "sacrifice" of OFWs. As I have discussed above, these are terms that resonate with a widely shared cultural and religious idiom in which a Filipino brand of heroism and idealized constructions of Christlike sacrifice are two sides of the same coin. Throughout the 1980s and 1990s, the discourse of the suffering hero-martyr became naturalized and, according to Jean Franco's (2011, 2) study, "endlessly repeated and widely disseminated across the media to the point that values, beliefs, and logics underlying the discourse are taken for granted in society at large." Its prevalence can be appreciated by the extent to which it figures in the way OFWs describe the broader applicability of their ritual agency, even outside of ritual domains, as Sencho has explained.

On June 21, 1988, two months after her Hong Kong speech, President Aquino issued Proclamation No. 276, which established the bagong bayani awards, an accolade meant to "underscore the emerging form of heroism which could only be attributed to the overseas contract workers' consistent contribution to the country's foreign exchange earnings and the efforts in employment generation" (BBF 2015). Bagong bayani were now formally lauded for the economic returns of their efforts, with the president proclaiming that, by and large, the economy benefited most from their sacrifice (Tigno 2012, 25–26). In this vein, the awards form part of the state's regime of governmentality in which a wide range of mechanisms—institutional, structural, and discursive—are deployed to not only regulate the mobility of working bodies but also to valorize them as "moral neoliberals" (Muehlebach 2012) who work for the well-being of their loved ones amid great physical and emotional tribulation.

Aquino's conflation of the economic and soteriological returns of overseas labor is an ethos that, to be sure, seeks to perpetuate the inward flow of foreign capital through the systematic and sustained deployment of productive transnational agents. Just as significantly, it is a religious ethic in which the pursuit of capital is seen as a form of both ethical and pious virtue—an association that is rationalized through rhetorical endorsements of sacrifice as a positive value. However, as opposed to what Max Weber ([1905] 2002) described as a Protestant ethic that extolls the virtue of frugality and financial reticence, the OFWs are lauded as heroic sufferers in generating capital and are encouraged to partake in modes of virtuous hyperconsumption. As Filomeno Aguilar (1999, 98) puts it, this is a form of transnational religious agency that is sustained by the "balm of commodities and the consumption of modernity."

For the past few decades, the export of labor has proven a significant source of revenue for the Philippines. The country ranks among the highest exporters of foreign labor in the world, and the trends have seen a steady increase during the past forty years (IOM 2013). There are more than ten million OFWs around the world (CFO 2012), with 2012 official surveys estimating their rate of remittances as high as US$21.39 billion (Alegado 2013; Ericta 2013). The rationale behind this burgeoning remittance economy is founded on the historically contingent Washington-consensus premise, which views the accumulation of foreign capital as the key to national social development and thus mandates the government to facilitate supporting institutional mechanisms (Williamson 1990).[4]

As such, the rhetorical force of Aquino's statement relied on the implication that OFWs were not forcibly driven out by a systematic failure of domestic governance but were instead virtuous individuals voluntarily pursuing their vocations in an open, democratic labor market. And while Aquino linked these pursuits with the prospect of religious transcendence in the afterlife, it was simultaneously a reiteration of the state's ideological promise that overseas work would yield material and economic reward in this life, provided that OFWs maintained their roles as drivers of the remittance economy.

The conflation of the material and soteriological returns of overseas labor, one that forms the basis of a Filipino brand of Catholicized neoliberalism, is premised on OFWs voluntarily devoting themselves to the pursuit of capital. Anthropologist Andrea Muehlebach (2013, 461) describes a market-driven welfare system that depends on the volition of "hypermoralized" neoliberals who operationalize the virtues of love, caritas, and volunteerism in the domestic economy in Lombardy, Italy. In the Filipino setting, Catholicized neoliberalism makes for an ethic whose agents are lauded for their willing capacity to channel their sacrifice into modes of transnational labor power, which the state monetizes for the greater good of the nation. The extent to which this monetization can be justified relies on the state's obfuscation of its own role in contributing to the volatility of transnational work and in the failure to mitigate the need for labor export in the first place (Franco 2011; Tadiar 2009; Tyner 2000). This obfuscation, more significantly, can be achieved only if the casualties of overseas labor are valorized as paragons of the highest civic and pious virtues.

The economy of sacrifice is sustained not just through a conflation of patriotism and martyrdom but through actual corporeal regimes as well. This occurs as part of a process of "labor brokerage," which, following Filipino/a studies scholars Anna Romina Guevarra (2010) and Robyn Rodriguez (2006, 2010), refers to the activities of nongovernmental institutions working in concert with the state in molding OFW bodies into productive economic units. This involves, among other things, the regimented implementation of body techniques, through which OFWs have been trained to deploy certain ethical and moral values about Christian self-effacement and humility onto translational domains. As part of these techniques, the institutions of labor brokerage provide predeparture assessment, training, and certification for would-be overseas workers to help them succeed in the economy of sacrifice. The training provided, however, is not merely the imparting of job-specific skills and knowledge to the prospective OFW but also the inculcation of certain attitudes and dispositions in the application of those skills. Most often, this involves specific bodily disciplines that encourage OFWs to physically deploy acts of self-regulation and self-effacement. For example, in the predeployment phase of marketing, female applicants are taught to adopt specific bodily postures—hands folded, head slightly bowed, and holding neutral, reticent expressions (Franco 2011, 53). Such programs are designed to enhance the export-competitiveness of Filipino OFWs, fashioning them into transnational agents who have been trained to externalize moral values and comportments of docility and subservience in the pursuit of overseas work.

The experience of Sencho as a practitioner of pagdarame (self-flagellation) who is also an OFW would seem to corroborate the efficacy of this discourse. While the ritual itself is performed only during Holy Week, the affective outcomes of pagdarame are not restricted to the temporal and geographical milieu of its performance. Sencho identified the practice of flagellation as that which imbued OFWs like him with a particular kind of inner fortitude (lakas ng loob) to confront the challenges of overseas work. "The [pre-departure] training was okay," says Sencho, as he described the years before his work in Saudi, "but it's a good thing that I've been doing flagellation for years—you learn to have confidence and lakas ng loob. You know, in a way, being an OFW is just like flagellation," he said, "you have to be disciplined and committed to finish it to the end, even though it hurts. In the end, God will answer your suffering by benefiting your family." While labor brokerage involves the disciplining of bodies for the purposes of maximizing their economic capacity, in Sencho's case, it was thinking about transnational labor as an extension of flagellation that enabled him to confront the harsh demands of the OFW experience. Given that his ritual agency was a form of empowerment, it would be inaccurate to assume that his export-quality martyrdom constituted a curbing, if not complete loss, of agency as stipulated by his brokers. The lakas ng loob that enabled him to persevere was not derived from embodying docility and subservience but rather from his previous experience of ritual performance—particularly, of pain infliction—that emboldened the confrontation with the demands of labor brokerage.

Lakas ng loob in this case is, as Michel Foucault has put it in *A History of Sexuality* ([1978] 1990, 141), an "investment of the body, its valorization, and the distributive management of its forces" toward the cultivation of what I would term "export-quality matyrs"—agents of transnational capital whose tradable labor power is premised upon their embodiment of the Christian virtue of willing, servile obedience. Export-quality martyrs are transnational economic agents trained to internalize and deploy modes of ethical docility toward what is promoted as the martyric pursuit of both spiritual and economic ends. The Philippine state cultivates this idea of productive, ethical transnationalism in the explicit linkage of the sacrifice of OFWs with the legacy of exemplary hero-martyrs. The corporeal dimension of this linkage is manifested in embodied comportments of self-discipline, both in the performance of rituals of flagellation and those acts and sensibilities inculcated in the process of recruitment and predeployment training.

In the state's co-option of culturally resonant themes of sacrifice and suffering, the bagong bayani discourse serves to obfuscate the dehumanizing volatility of transnational labor and the role the state plays in propagating it. The valorization of new heroes, especially when they fall victim to the perilousness of transnational labor, is characterized as the unfortunate but necessary cost of pursuing a greater good. For to "suffer" in overseas labor is to inherit the legacy of fallen martyrs—from Rizal to Aquino, from Siosin to Contemplacion. The voluntary placing of the body in harm's way is more than just a metaphor. The OFW body, though it may well evoke sentiments of pity, is an actual testament to patriotism of the highest order. It makes sense that the state expands its resources toward the cultivation of these export-oriented bodies.

Suffering Martyrdom

The most revered heroes in the Philippines are not those who led armed revolutions or strategized the overthrow of tyrants. If we go by the ideological currency, modern heroes are those who knew that they would suffer physically and emotionally in their pursuit of difficult working conditions, and yet willingly and knowingly subjected themselves to it. In this chapter I have argued that both the Roman Catholic Church and the Philippine state have played significant roles in propagating this notion by cultivating the idea of "suffering missionaries" and "export quality martyrs." Perhaps ironically, the pervasiveness of the discourse that extols the religious and patriotic normativity of suffering is contingent on a reframing of the meaning of sacrifice itself. In this reframing, OFW martyrdom is not oriented toward a perfect mimesis of the life trajectories of fallen OFWs. To give one's life—an act traditionally considered a prerequisite to heroism and martyrdom—has been taken out of the equation in the fulfillment of the OFW's act of suffering.

Epilogue
Suffering, Personhood, and Christendom's Changing Face

The problematic that frames this ethnography is that our capacity to understand the rationale behind self-inflicted ritual pain is diminished by our visceral aversion to pain, even when experienced vicariously. This aversion is conditioned by and further exacerbated by two different paradigms: on the one hand, an epicurean and biomedical paradigm that has naturalized the notion that pain is amenable to domestication through treatment and avoidance and, on the other, a Christian theological paradigm that stipulates the soteriological redundancy of physically experiencing divine suffering. I have addressed this problematic by discussing the various ritual manifestations of a counterintuitive idea—that it is precisely because of pain, experienced and felt through the emotional wellsprings that undergird life's suffering, that ritual agents are able to craft modes of positive religious personhood from painful ritual expressions.

Although they each manifest distinct procedural features, the three Passion rituals that I have examined in this book are united in one crucial aspect: far from being the repressive modes of confessional self-denial that missionaries intended them to be, they are attempts at crafting a specific kind of suffering selfhood, premised upon the acknowledgment that the body is the primary vehicle toward religious and material well-being. Well-being, as it is conceived in the course of Passion rituals, is not tantamount to the achievement of atonement for sins or access to union with God in the hereafter. The pursuit of well-being, rather, is predicated upon the ritual agent's "interbeing" with a "community of sufferers." Horizontally framed in this way, pious agency in all three rituals resides in the ability to anticipate and elicit divine reciprocation in ways that are meaningful because they proceed from exemplary corporeal and emotional exertion.

In examining how intersubjective ontologies of suffering are crafted in the course of painful rituals, what I offer in this final section is not a conclusion per se but a postscript that points to the analytical and discursive currents within which this examination of suffering selfhood can be situated. From the perspective of the anthropology of religion, I contribute to the range of cross-cultural ethnographies that critique the conception of personhood as an individualist, "buffered" subjectivity, in which there is a keen awareness of the boundaries between the "self" and others (C. Taylor 2007). Suffering selfhoods in Pampanga can be situated within a distinct anthropological tradition, formulated most prominently in the writings of Marilyn Strathern (1988), Roy Wagner (1991) and Alfred Gell ([1998] 2013), which conceives of persons as defined by the intersubjective, interpersonal bonds that they enter into, thereby emphasizing the "partible," "composite," or "distributed" nature of human subjectivity. Roman Catholic ritual practitioners in Pampanga are "dividuals" who, as Strathern (1988, 13) has observed in Malenesia, are persons who are "frequently constructed as the plural and composite site of the relationships that produce them." More recently, anthropologists working under the rubric of New Melanesian Ethnography have been at the forefront of examining the ramifications of dividual personhood for Christian subjectivity. Sabine Hess (2006) and Mark Mosko (2010) have been among those who have described the salient features of an intersubjective, horizontal orientation of dividual personhood. "[By] entering into an exchange relationship with God," observes Hess (2006, 294), "one becomes part of Him, and He becomes part of oneself." This book has been an examination of the different facets of this kind of partible personhood. In Pampanga, the dividuality of suffering selfhood is manifested in at least three ways (which correspond to the three thematic currents I have postulated in the introduction): (1) in the adoption or reconfiguration of discursive and ideological missionary inheritances, (2) in the embeddedness of divine intimacy in the ritual investment in social relationships, and (3) in how agentive subjects confront the varied demands and challenges presented by modern institutional forces. Below I revisit some of the important points made in each chapter in a way that places emphasis on suffering selfhood as a mode of intersubjective personhood.

In the first chapter, I traced the ideologies that have conditioned a particular understanding of "suffering" among Roman Catholics in the Philippines. The starting point of this discussion was the idea that suffering selfhood draws contiguous corporeal acts of ascetic self-denial, which became a basis for the achievement of spiritual transcendence among medieval monastics in Europe. That European ascetic practices were transplanted in non-Western worlds might seem at odds with the fact that contemporary ritual practitioners hardly ever associate their practice with this lineage. What I have tried to establish, however, is not that contemporary rituals are direct survivals of imposed practices but rather the ideological and discursive continuity of Christianity's subjectifying capacity. What has continued to the present is not so much the corporeal manifestation of the pursuit of self-denial and transcendence. Rather, what we find today are traces of what anthropologist Jon Bialecki calls a mode of intersubjective subject formation that can be described as "dividual" in that "one does extensive self-work that presumes a certain autonomy and control of one's person, but which is undertaken in furtherance of a more intimate relationship with God" (Bialecki 2015).

From the second chapter onward, I sought to examine the embodied ritual manifestations of suffering selfhood as dividual subjectivity. This began, in chapter two, with a discussion of the *pabasa* as a state of being "ensounded" in a sensorium of sensual bereavement for Christ, itself made more meaningful in the ritual agent's efforts to collectively "suffer through" the strain of vocalizing vernacular religious texts. As in the first chapter, I sought to acknowledge the historicity the contemporary ritual practice in vernacular religious texts introduced by Spanish missionaries as a contingency to the eventual prohibition of corporeal rituals by secular authorities. I have argued that the sorrowful energies projected by those who conduct the pabasa produce a horizontally projected emotional contagion that, in turn, conditions the pious itineraries of other Passion ritual practitioners as they traverse the provincial landscape during Holy Week. We see again, therefore, that the suffering selfhoods that are aurally channeled in the sound of chanting cultivate dividual Christian personhoods in those who are within the voice's acoustic range.

In the third and fourth chapters, I paid close attention to the sentiments that motivate and sustain rituals of self-flagellation and ritual nailing, respectively. It is important to underscore that although they differ in form and application, the practitioners of both these ritual acts call forth a connection between interiorized subjectivity, or *lub,* and the sentiments and emotions of pity, empathy, and trust that are shared by a community of sufferers during Holy Week. Drawing from this, the main thrust of this second theme—that of investments—is that ritual commemoration of Christ's suffering should be understood as part of an ensemble of intersubjective orientations that goes beyond an individualist, inward cultivation of belief. In this sense, both self-flagellants and ritual nailers cultivate a special connection with one's interbeings, or *kapwa,* and with God, with whom one becomes intimate enough to receive divine favor.

There are two aspects of the ritual experience in Pampanga that contribute to our understanding of dividual personhood. First, as I discussed in chapter 3, the triangulated empathy that is crafted by ritual self-flagellants combines a supplicatory and interecessionary mode of divine communion. More than an expression of consociation with Christ's own suffering, it is also a somewhat paradoxical appeal for the subject of empathy to validate the commensurability between the empathizer's pain and his worthiness to receive material benefit on behalf of a suffering third party. Secondly, as I showed in chapter 4, the *tiala ya lub* (trust) that facilitates the act of ritual nailing channels a complementarity of interior states between the ritual agent and his trusted ritual collaborator. This complementarity can only be predicated upon the porosity of interior states, a porosity that involves the volitional extension of interiority toward an intersubjective relationship with a trusted intersubject. In both cases, flagellants and nailees are agents who manage plural and intersecting identities in the course of their embodied ritual activities. The pursuit of Passion rituals emphasizes distinct dividual personhoods—those who, in the course of the pain experience, extend themselves to others and to God.

Acknowledging that the ritual cultivation of dividual personhood is historically contingent and complex, the last part of this ethnography was devoted to how ritual enactments of suffering articulate with or challenge contemporary, "modern" discursive, theological, and institutional formations. In the last two chapters, I directed the ethnographic data toward a consideration of how religious and state bureaucracies condition corporeal manifestations of suffering selfhood, particularly as it extends outside of the ritual domains of Pampanga.

In the fifth chapter, I discussed the seeming tension between Passion ritual practitioners, and clerical "gatekeepers" in the Philippine Roman Catholic Church. I argued that there is a multifaceted range of clerical perspectives on Passion rituals, and that these perspectives should not be reduced to the voices of condemnation or disavowal that tend to dominate the public persecution of Passion rituals. Seeking a more nuanced institutional perspective, I aligned the spectrum of clerical responses within an a rubric of "inculturation"—a Church-endorsed ethical framework in which Gospel truth is made to reconcile with the extraliturgical realities of Roman Catholic personhood. I have shown that it is within this incultured framework that Passion ritual practitioners are able to position their ritual agency within some form of institutional adherence.

In the sixth chapter, I focused on how the Philippine state's bureaucratic apparatus extolls an explicit linkage between the suffering of overseas Filipino workers (OFWs) and the legacy of exemplary Filipino hero-martyrs. This is done in order to depict OFWs circulation and survival in a harsh world oriented toward global flows of labor and capital as both desirable and ideal. Correspondingly, the overarching theme that is evoked in the ethnographic cases I discussed is how engaging in ritual is thought to be meaningful because it provides people with the moral, ethical, and sentimental wellsprings from which they draw as they face the vicissitudes and ruptures of modernity. One central observation I made was that the personhood of Filipino Catholics, particularly those who are working overseas, is founded on the same sentimental architecture of suffering selfhood that drives the performance of Passion rituals.

This ethnography of Passion rituals has been a way to confront the deficits in our existing religious vocabularies pertaining to suffering and the way it conditions intersubjective personhood. This notion might initially be difficult to accept because of a persistent epicurean assumption that anything that involves pain cannot be constitutive of rational, self-conscious social agents. The clinical view of pain, which remains prevalent in a modern society oriented toward epicurean pursuits, leaves little room for appreciating how pain can facilitate the formation of religious and social selfhoods. While ritual practitioners commonly described the physical sensation of their rituals in terms of "relief" and "release," this does not mean that there is no pain, or that ritual protagonists experience states of trance or desensitization. Rather, the physical strain on the body is interpreted within a rubric of suffering selfhood that is coterminous—even equivalent—with the facilitation of one's capacity to pursue well-being for oneself and those one cares about.

In analyzing the rituals of *pabasa, pagdarame,* and *pamamaku king krus*— all of which are complex ways in which people in Pampanga craft their suffering selfhood and orient their ritual practice toward spiritual and material upliftment—this ethnography advances the discursive move away from the trope of Christian exceptionalism to a more nuanced acknowledgement of Christian particularity. The anthropologist Fenella Cannell (2006) has pointed out that anthropology's initial fixation on "primitive" societies had once precluded a self-reflexive focus on the study of the diversity of Christian lifeworlds, including the modes of personhood that are cultivated in ritual practice. This ethnography, however, unfolds in a vastly different context that has been building for at least the past three decades. A host of anthropological works have subsequently emerged out of the discipline's initial reluctance to examine its own inheritance, emphasizing instead an analytic openness to the vibrancy of Christian ritual practice in contexts outside of its traditional Western bastions.

This resurgent and vibrant academic interest in non-Western Christianity has coincided with Christianity's "changing face," premised upon a major demographic shift of Christendom toward the Global South (Jenkins 2002; Sanneh and Carpenter 2005). This is not just a demographic issue about changing patterns of where Christians live. Given the declining rates of adherence in Europe and North America, there is a very real sense that the continuance of the Christian faith will largely be determined by the dynamism of ritual practice and subject formation in places such as the Philippines, Nigeria, Mexico, and Papua New Guinea. I think it is important because what Roman Catholics do, feel, or say in non-Western domains—regardless of how "radical," "literalist," or "excessive" it may seem to religious orthodoxies—may eventually constitute "the new normal" of the faith going forward into the next millennium.

Introduction

1. All those who trace their cultural and ethnic lineage to the province of Pampanga generally refer to themselves as "Kapampangans" (variously referred to as Pampangans or Pampangeños), who form the sixth-largest ethnolinguistic group in the Philippines.

2. Around two-thirds of the 124 million Christians in Southeast Asia are Catholics, and about 90 percent of them live in only two countries: the Philippines and Indonesia. While most Christians in the world (90 percent) live as religious majorities in their countries, in Southeast Asia only in the Philippines and, very recently, in Timor Leste, do Christians make up the dominant faith (Pew Forum 2011).

3. The Philippine census of 2015 indicates that the province of Pampanga has a population of 2,198,110 in a total land area of 2,062.47 square kilometers. The primary location of this research, the provincial capital city of San Fernando, has a population of 306,659 as indicated in the 2015 census, up from 285,915 in 2010 (Pangilinan 2015). The population of San Pedro Cutud, a town within San Fernando, is 12,219 as of 2015. Pampanga, with its present boundaries as established in 1873, belongs to the third national administrative region of Central Luzon, bordered to the north by Ilocos and the Cagayan Valley; to the south by the National Capital Region; and to the west and east by the South China Sea and the Philippine Sea, respectively. Pampanga remains one of the provinces that form what is known as the "rice granary of the Philippines," producing most of the country's rice supply (Ericta 2010).

4. The Philippines, in fact, leads the world in surveys about belief, such as the one taken in 2012 by the National Opinion Research (NOR) Center at the University of Chicago (T. Smith 2012). In a sample involving over thirty countries in Europe, the United States and Asia, the NOR survey found that 93.5 percent of Filipinos professed "I believe in God now and I always have," while 91.9 percent declared a belief in a personal God. In all, 60.2 percent of those surveyed are "certain God exists, always believed in God, and strongly agree that there is a personal God." This is the highest among the surveyed countries, the next being Israel with 38 percent, and the United States with 35 percent. Correspondingly, the Philippines is at the bottom of the list of patterns of nonbelief. Only 0.1 percent of Filipinos "Don't believe in God; Never believed in God, and Strongly disagree that there is a personal God" (T. Smith 2012, 8–11). This is corroborated by local accounts. A Philippines Social Weather Station (SWS) survey conducted in February 2013 asked 1,200 participants to respond to the statement "Sometimes I think I might leave the Catholic Church." The survey report, however, put an over-alarmist focus on those who would "strongly agree" (a mere 2.5 percent) and "somewhat agree" (6.7 percent). This emphasis seems heavily misplaced, given that the percentage of those who would "somewhat disagree" (11.4) alone outnumbers the combined total of the two affirmative categories. This is not even considering that over-whelming majority of respondents, or 74.2 percent, would "strongly disagree" with the statement. By an objective measure, the survey indicated a strong adherence to the faith corresponding to an increasing population.

5. To give a sense of the timeframe in which Passion rituals have been studied, the following scholars are worth mentioning. Among anthropologists, Fernando Zialcita (1986, 2000) has classified thirty-four cases of flagellation, crucifixion, and other Lenten rituals (1986, 57); Nicholas Barker (1998) conducted fieldwork in San Pedro Cutud during Lent in 1984, 1987, and 1988, and for more extended periods in 1990, 1991, and 1998 (1998, 26); and Peter Bräunlein (2009, 2010a, 2010b) conducted research in Kapitagan, Bulacan, between 1996 and 1998. Theatre studies scholars Sir Anril Tiatco and Amihan Bonifacio-Ramolete (2008) interviewed four nailees between 2004 and 2005, while other unpublished works on Passion rituals include those of Alison Murray (1988), and Cuyno, Gutierrez, and Takeno (2005). Finally, the work of theatre studies scholar William Peterson (2016) has contributed greatly to our understanding of the Passion rituals by discussing the pursuit of "happiness" through "community-based performance practices" in the central Philippines.

Chapter 1: The Ideology of Suffering Selfhood in Medieval and Colonial Domains

1. Scholastic interest in the humanity and corporality of Christ corresponded with increasing knowledge about the workings and capacities of the human body from the thirteenth century. Several scholars have analyzed the development of Christianity through a consideration of corporeality and embodiment. See Rubin 1991; Trembinski 2008.

2. John Paul II had declared that he found inspiration from the ascetic practices of the Carmelite monastic order, who would flog themselves with the sashes of their cassocks. As the Catholic historian Michael Walsh (2010, 46) argues, "The Vatican body . . . would regard [John Paul II's flagellation] as a sign of his religious commitment." John Paul II wrote an Apostolic Letter titled "Salvifici Doloris," in which he sought to "to understand the salvific meaning of suffering" by associating it with the fundamental Christian principle of redemption. In Pope John Paul's view, Christianity is founded upon the very redemption that comes through an appreciation for God-in-pain, such that, as Ariel Glucklich (2001, 4) puts it, "pain and suffering are not simply to be overcome, but are central to salvation."

3. To cite only a few notable examples, Francis of Assisi (1181/1182–1226) had named his body "Brother Ass," according to his biographer, Thomas of Celano (2000), since he treated it as harshly as a peasant would a donkey by rolling in snow or thorns whenever he felt tempted by women. Like Francis, Beatrice of Ornacieux (1240–1306/1309) would also stride barefoot in the snow to quell the torment of the devil, and was said by her biographer, Margaret D'Oingt (1990, 49), to have "evoked the Passion of our Lord so strongly that she pierced her hands with blunt nails until it came out at the back of her hand. And every time she did this, clear water without any blood in it gushed out." She is, as such, depicted in a thirteenth-century painting by Daniele Crespi as clasping a hammer and a nail. Mother Teresa of Calcutta (1910–1997) used a spiked garter called a cilice, as did Saint Pio (Pius) of Pietrelcina, O.F.M. Cap., (May 25, 1887—September 23, 1968), and Óscar Arnulfo Romero y Galdámez (August 15, 1917—March 24, 1980) For an account of other saintly exemplars who conducted pious acts of pain infliction, see Fredricks (2012) and Baab (2006).

4. There are other biblical references to self-mortification. In Colossians 3:5, the community of faith are instructed, "Mortify therefore your members which are upon the earth; fornication, uncleanness, lust, evil concupiscence, and covetousness, which is the service of idols." This was preceded in the Old Testament by acts of mortification among

the Chosen people, as indicated in Genesis 37:34; 1 Kings 21:27–29; Joel 1:13–14; Isaiah 22:12–14.

5. While Saint Pardulf (657–ca. 737), an abbot in Aquitaine, is recognized as an early adopter of flogging (Bräunlein 2010b), Saint Damian is important because he had successfully incorporated self-flagellation as an institutionalized monastic routine. The physical and mental regimes that Damian inculcated sought to harness the body's full sensual and affective range to cultivate a heightened sense of divine intimacy and community.

6. By the thirteenth century, observes anthropologist Peter Bräunlein (2010b, 1120), "self-inflicted suffering became increasingly appreciated by the religious virtuoso." German Dominicans, notably Heinrich Seuse (1295/1297–1366), Elsbeth von Oye (1290–1340), and Margareta Ebner (1291–1351), practiced similarly gruesome forms of self-mortification, of which self-flagellation "constituted the rather 'harmless' component" (Bräunlein 2010b, 1120). Meanwhile, according to Norman Cohn (1970, 27), acts of disciplina spread rapidly until it became "not only a normal feature of monastic life throughout Latin Christendom but the commonest form of all penitential techniques."

7. Carolyn Brewer (2004, 73) observes from reading the colonial archives that the participation of women in public displays of flagellation was relatively unusual, although not because they were forbidden or precluded from the practice. "While men flagellated en masse under the watchful eye of the priest and before the assembled faithful, women were encouraged to take the discipline individually in the privacy of their own homes and in isolation from each other."

8. The reforms involved a significant reduction in the power and operational capacities of clerical orders. For example, the Jesuits, who were among the more ardent supporters of rituals of self-mortification, were suppressed in 1767. The reforms also called for tighter regulation, and at times suppression, of religious cofradias, which were often the context in which Eucharistic plays, liturgical dances, pilgrimages, and flagellant processions were conducted (Sapitula 2013, 104–105).

9. The Spanish reforms of the public practice of religious rituals were likewise implemented in Spanish America, particularly in Mexico, where elaborate and overly demonstrative commemorations of the Passion were discouraged or banned (Carroll 2002, 85).

Chapter 2: The Ensounded Body

1. Versions of the pasyon exist in vernaculars other than Kapampangan, including Bisaya, Bikolano, Ilokano, Hiligaynon, Tagalog, and Ibanag. This reflects the commitment Spanish missionaries placed on the pasyon as a vernacular tool. See Lumbera (1986).

2. Nathan Porath (2008, 649) has the most nuanced definition of sound as a cultivator of awareness. By "sound" he means "A particular type of sensory patterning momentarily constituting part of the body's awareness, which is either stimulated by a particular band of (sound) waves (sound frequencies) in the external environment or projected onto the body's perceptual awareness by its own re-configurations (consciousness)."

3. Although clerics did take this flexible approach, they did not always have complete control over how the pabasa was read, or indeed what meanings native converts derived from it. Regarding the clerically transcribed pabasa, Father De Zuñiga observed that converts "do not wish to read it but rather other Pasiones, which they have made themselves, full of fables, which they like very much because they emphasize the marvelous" (Schumacher 1979, 179). He goes on to say, "Despite their harmless nature, many parish priests forbid them to read them, because besides the foolishness which is

found in them, the young men and women often make use of the pretext of reading the Passion in order to make love to each other" (179). The scholar Mirano notes an incident in 1827 in which a Spanish parish priest complained about "erroneous doctrinal ideas being spread by such [vocalized readings]" (Mirano 1992, 14; see also Irving 2010, 152). Similarly, Dominican priest Jun Lopez describes natives who "are prone to singing dirty songs, with one intoning [the key and verse] and everyone else continuing the song by responding to each verse" (quoted in Lumbera 1986, 35; see also Blanco 2009, 104). Incidents such as these were more than just symptoms of an inadequately internalized doctrinal message. As Ileto has argued, these pabasa gatherings provided the occasion for peasants to craft their own interpretations of religious texts, based on their own ideals and internalized values, that eventually formed the basis for mass movements that challenged the colonial order (Ileto 1979, 59). The penetration and widespread adoption of the pabasa enabled lowland converts to think of Christ's "suffering" in ways that prefigured religiously inspired postcolonial independence movements of the late nineteenth century. The intervention of charismatic leaders was crucial to this cooptation of the pabasa and other evangelical strategies. Much like how the early Church fathers reworked the meaning of punishment toward a renewed ideology of victorious martyrdom, religious leaders in Pampanga such as Felipe Salvador channeled the "suffering selfhood" emphasized in the pasyon to enjoin supporters to defy Spanish colonial authority. They turned pabasa sessions into opportunities to reiterate the link between Christ's "suffering" and that of their own in a way that resonated with the struggle against social injustice. Further emboldened by the use of amulets and talismanic objects, the pasyon fueled a revolution that derived its impetus in and through the very narrative and idiom of subjugation.

4. Ric Trimillos (1992) notes that the Lunas Bookstore of Manila is the major publisher of the "Pasiung Pilapil," having facilitated its translations into Bikolano, Kapampangan, Ilocano, and Ilonggo.

5. This structure is quite common in the Philippines, variously referred to as Kapilya, *grotto* (grave), or *kubol* (tomb) (Trimillos 1992; Bautista 2010).

6. In fact, as Trimillos (1992, 9) has observed, the pabasa "is not to be performed where the Host is located."

7. It is not uncommon for sponsors to "import" noteworthy singers from other towns to perform. The evening sessions are especially crucial in this regard, although Trimillos has observed that it is at this time that the "imported" performers take their turns, allowing the family to rest. But on this occasion, Aling Cel and her family have taken a "hands-on" approach, and they do the chant.

8. R. Collins (2004, 51) describes failed rituals as gatherings that have " little or no feeling of group solidarity; no sense of one's identity as affirmed or changed; no respect for the group's symbols; no heightened emotional energy—either a flat feeling unaffected by the ritual, or worse yet, a sense of a drag, the feeling of boredom and constraint, even depression, interaction fatigue, a desire to escape."

9. As opposed to what Schafer's notion of "soundscape" would posit, the technological enhancements do not diminish its efficacy. It is indeed significant that the pabasa is tape-recorded by one of the householders. I was told that the recordings are sent to relatives overseas, particularly those who have sent money to sponsor the costs of holding the pabasa for the community. It is in one respect a gesture of gratitude for their contributions. The family also expressed hope that the recorded sessions would help their relatives in their own life struggles—a reminder that their suffering in overseas domains, as with Christ's own, is noble. Technology facilitates the family's capacity to

effectively extend the reach of sonic piety, transmuting it to a broader audience even though they are beyond immediate space and time. Technology is seen as a vehicle of affect, furnishing the family with the ability to reproduce the kind of aural conditions that would encourage the same modes of religious inspiration that mourners in the puni share. Technology is a medium of sonic piety because it enables he transmission of metasignals—sounds that functioning indexically to recreate the affect of bereavement, effectively extending the pabasa chanter's "inner self in good faith to others" (*nag mamagandang loob sa kapwa*).

10. Both Ric Trimillos (1992) and Fenella Cannell (1995) observe that the intensity of participatory interest corresponds with certain sections that depict the religious significance of the Passion narrative.

11. The pabasa operates in the way that the anthropologist Greg Urban (1988, 392) describes as characteristic of ritual wailing: "It is intended not to be heard, in the ordinary linguistic sense, but rather to be overheard." Similarly, the anthropologist A. R. Radcliffe-Brown (1964, 239–240) observed that ritual weeping among the Andaman islanders was more than a personal expression of sorrow; it was also a ceremonial practice wherein "men and women are required by custom to embrace one another and weep." He argued that the purpose of the latter form was, to quote Urban (1988, 385), "to affirm the existence of a social bond between two or more persons," which is itself a function of the emotions projected and externalized by weeping and wailing.

12. Listening presupposes an intentionality of acquiring the content of what is being delivered. Listeners seek to receive and decipher what is being preached, prompting a process of deliberation. Listening activities require some degree of concentration so that one processes the sounds from spoken words and sentences.

13. In his ethnography of ritual wailing in Amerindian Brazil, Urban (1988, 385) argues that "ritual wailing functions simultaneously on two planes: (1) the plane of overt expression of emotion, in this case, the feeling of sadness at separation or death; and (2) the plane of covert expression of the desire for sociability." This analysis transposes well with what I have observed in Pampanga, as well as with what Filipino philosophers, historians, and anthropologists have written.

14. Charles Hirschkind (2006) describes the "ethical soundscape" created by Islamic sermon tapes in Cairo. He is concerned with describing how sermons of well-known Muslim preachers have an ubiquity that defines the aural landscape of both private and public domains, creating sounds that "spill onto the street from loudspeakers in cafes, the shops of tailors and butchers, the workshop of mechanics and TV repairmen . . . where men and women listen alone in the privacy of their homes after returning home from the factory" (7). Hirschkind does not think of the sound of broadcast tapes as a dystopian "soundscape," as it is conceptualized by Schafer. Far from noise pollution, rather, he argues that the tapes are a way for Egyptians to acquire the religious knowledge and sensibilities necessary to act ethically in a rapidly changing social and political environment. To be sure, many preachers who produce these tapes use it as an opportunity to discuss contemporary political issues that affect Muslims, but this is done in a way that evokes the Islamic tradition of aural sensibility and discipline in a format that is cathartic, soothing, and educational. Indeed, sermon tapes are "attended to in a relaxed manner, often with shifting degrees of focus," and in that sense are an "ethically enhancing form of relaxation" (82).

15. Soundscape has been used widely to denote virtually any scenario that involves both sound as constitutive of lived experience and the analytical heuristics that could be used to understand those experiences. More recently, however, there has been

some push-back on the concept, most prominently by Tim Ingold (2011), who cautioned against abstracting the senses into discreet modes of perception, thereby obfuscating the experiential component of aurality. Those such as A. V. Kelman (2010), moreover, have suggested that we need to be more attentive to the ideologically dystopian aspect of Schafer's concept which, in its original, lamented how "harmonious" sounds of nature had become eroded by the artificial cacophonies of modern life. "Schafer's soundscape is not a neutral field of aural investigation at all," Kelman (2010, 214) points out; "rather, it is deeply informed by Schafer's own preferences for certain sounds over others. The soundscape is a prescriptive text that is often referred to as a descriptive one."

Chapter 4: The Way of the Cross

1. The province of Pampanga at the turn of the twentieth century had a spirited theatrical fervor that gives us the creative milieu in which the first staging of the Via Crucis was embedded. The rich tradition of vernacular theatre, which has a long history in Pampanga, can be seen most prominently with the vernacularization of the *zarzuela*, a genre of lyric drama featuring both spoken and sung scenes, dance and operatic music introduced by Spanish colonizers in the sixteenth century. The first vernacular zarzeula, *Ing Managpe* (The patcher) was first conceived on the premises of the Kapampangan justice Jose Gutierrez David, later opening to much fanfare in September 1900 in the Teatro Sabina, which staged an average of two productions a month. A slew of drama troupes were established, among them, Compania Paz, Compania Ocampo in Candaba, Compania Dramatica in Bacolor, and Compania Lubeña in Lubao; in 1901, the Teatro Trining in Guagua staged a three-act zarzuela, *Ing Mangaibugan* (The greedy one).

2. There is a significant degree of animosity between the official and unofficial towns designated for pamamaku sponsorship. During the city government's 2010 planning meetings, which I attended, for example, Captain Aldana of San Juan town had accused those in the other towns of attempting to "pirate" their Kristos, or *"namamakus"* (personal field notes, March 10, 2010).

3. I describe the circumstances and experience of this in Bautista (2014).

4. I describe some of the perspectives of these other nailers in Bautista (2014).

5. The Augustinian friar Diego Bergaño, who wrote one of the earliest and most comprehensive dictionaries of Kapampangan terms in 1732, defined "lub" as "that which the root says, it is within the soul. . . . It is understood as the will, what he wants" (Bergaño [1732] 2007, 225–226).

6. The entrusted agency that I describe here resonates with the ideas of actor-network theorists, notably Bruno Latour (2005) and John Law and John Hassard (1999), who have critiqued the human-centeredness of agency and included animals and objects in its conceptual range (Enfield 2013, 116). Similarly, in *Art and Agency* ([1998] 2013), anthropologist Alfred Gell has argued that an individual who uses a tool or an object extends his agency across time and space. In that sense, objects are repositories of "distributed personhood" (21).

Chapter 5: Clerical Perspectives on Passion Rituals

This chapter is a significantly revised version of the article by J. Bautista, "On the Anthropology and Theology of Passion Rituals in the Roman Catholic Philippines," *International Journal of Asian Christianity* 1, no. 1 (January 2018): 143–156.

Chapter 6: Suffering Selfhood in Transnational Domains

1. Rhetorical endorsements of the positive value of sacrifice rationalize the cultivation of what I have termed "export-quality martyrs" (Bautista 2015), a designation that applies to those who steadfastly pursue their roles as critical agents of capital accumulation and who, in so doing, effectively contribute toward a collective, nationwide spiritual economy.

2. The most prominent institutions that fulfill this mandate include the Episcopal Commission for Migrants and Itinerant Peoples (ECMI), a nationwide network that operates under the auspices of the CBCP in providing pastoral care and social services to migrant workers. It is oriented toward the development and formation of OFWs to be witnesses of the Gospel in their foreign assignments. Similarly, the Apostleship of the Sea (AOS) is an organization run and headed by a Scalabrini priest that looks after the welfare of seafarers by coordinating support centers based in major cities in the Philippines. Finally, the Centre for Overseas Workers (COW), in operation since the early 1980s, is headed by Sr. Bernadette of the Religious of the Good Shepherd, and conducts daily Pre-Departure Orientation Seminars (PDOS) specifically for women bound for East and Southeast Asia. It also lobbies for workers rights through the legislative process.

3. To name but a few, there is Maricris Sioson, a twenty-two-year-old entertainer, who died in mysterious and contested circumstances in Japan in 1991, and Flor Contemplacion, a domestic helper in Singapore, who was tried, convicted, and later executed for double murder in spite of mitigating contrary evidence (Franco 2011, 140). Lastly, Angelo de la Cruz, a forty-four-year-old truck driver, was abducted in Iraq by militants demanding the country's withdrawal from the "Coalition of the Willing." De La Cruz was depicted by the Arroyo presidential press secretary as "a man kneeling with three masked men purportedly belonging to the Khaled Ibn al-Walid Brigade which has links to the Islamic Army in Iraq" (141).

4. Developments outside the Philippines, namely, the Middle East oil boom in the 1970s and the rapid growth of the East and Southeast Asian economies in the 1980s, opened up demand and opportunities for Filipino labor, particularly during the Marcos-era regime of "developmental authoritarianism" (Hau 2004, 230). By the late 1980s and early 1990s, the ostensibly temporary solution to the government's inability to formulate sound economic, political, and social solutions to poverty became a cornerstone of its development plans (231).

Abraham, Morris. 2002. "Taboo. Season 1 Episode 11: Tests of Faith." National Geographic TV, aired December 23.

Aguilar, Filomeno V. 1998. *Clash of Spirits: The History of Power and Sugar Planter Hegemony on a Visayan island*. Honolulu: University of Hawaiʻi Press.

——. 1999. "Ritual Passage and the Reconstruction of Selfhood in International Labor Migration." *Sojourn* 14 (1): 98–139.

Aguilar, Filomeno, John Peñalosa, Tania Liwanag, Resto Cruz, and Jimmy Melendrez. 2009. *Maalwang buhay: Family, Overseas Migration, and Cultures of Relatedness in Barangay Paraiso*. Quezon City, Philippines: Ateneo de Manila University Press.

Alegado, Siegfried. 2013. "Overseas Filipino Remittances Hit Record-High $2.062B in October." GMA News Online. December 16. http://www.gmanetwork.com.

Alejo, Albert. 1990. *Tao po! Tuloy!: Isang landas ng pag-unawa sa loob ng tao*. Quezon City, Philippines: Office of Research and Publications, Ateneo de Manila University.

Appell-Warren, Laura P. 2014. *Personhood: An Examination of the History and Use of an Anthropological Concept*. Lewiston, NY: Edwin Mellen.

Asad, Talal. 1973. *Anthropology and the Colonial Encounter*. New York: Humanities Press.

——. 1983. "Notes on Body Pain and Truth in Medieval Christian Ritual." *Economy and Society* 12:287–327.

——. 1987. "On Ritual and Discipline in Medieval Christian Monasticism." *Economy and Society* 16 (2): 159–203.

——. 1993. *Genealogies of Religion : Discipline and Reasons of Power in Christianity and Islam*. Baltimore, MD: Johns Hopkins University Press.

Asia News. 2004. " 'The Passion of the Christ': A Milestone in the Cinema History." *Asia News*. Accessed January 22, 2015. http://www.asianews.it.

Baab, Lynne M. 2006. *Fasting: Spiritual Freedom beyond Our Appetites*. Downers Grove, IL: IVP Books.

Badillo, Victor. 2010. "Export Quality Christians." *Pedro Calungsod*. August 6. Accessed July 4, 2014. http://pedrocalungsod.blogspot.sg/2010/08/export-quality.html.

Bagong Bayani Foundation (BBF). 2015. "Paying Tribute to OFWs." Accessed June 9, 2015. http://www.bbfi.com.ph.

Balsera, Viviana Díaz. 2005. *The Pyramid under the Cross: Franciscan Discourses of Evangelization and the Nahua Christian Subject in Sixteenth-Century Mexico*. Tucson: University of Arizona Press.

Barker, Nicholas H. 1998. "The Revival of Ritual Self-Flagellation and the Birth of Crucifixion in Lowland Christian Philippines." Nagoya University Graduate School of International Development, Discussion Paper (6) 3.

Barney, Lt. Charles. 1903. *Circumcision and Flagellation among the Filipinos*. Carlisle, PA: Association of Military Surgeons.

Barrion, M. Caridad. 1960. "Religious Life of the Laity in Eighteenth-Century Philippines Reflected in the Decrees of the Council of Manila of 1771 and the Synod of Calasiao of 1773." PhD diss., University of Santo Tomas, Manila.

Barrion, Maria Caridad. 1960. "Religious Life of the Laity in Eighteenth-Century Philippines as Reflected in the Decrees of the Council of Manila of 1771 and the Synod of Calasiao of 1773." PhD diss., University of Santo Tomas, Manila.

Bautista, Julius. 2010. *Figuring Catholicism: An Ethnohistory of the Santo Niño de Cebu.* Quezon City, Philippines: Ateneo de Manila University Press.

———. 2011. "The Bearable Lightness of Pain: Crucifying Oneself in Pampanga." In *Pain: Management, Expression and Interpretation,* edited by Andrzej Dańczak and Nicola Lazenby, 151–159. Oxford: Interdisciplinary Press.

———. 2014. "The Localization of Roman Catholicism: Radical Transcendence and Social Empathy in a Philippine Town." In *The Routledge Handbook of Asian Christianity,* edited by Oscar Salemink and Bryan Turner, 96–109. Oxford: Routledge.

———. 2015. "Export-Quality Martyrs: Roman Catholicism and Transnational Labor in the Philippines." *Cultural Anthropology* 30 (3): 424–447.

Beltran, Benigno. 1987. *The Christology of the Inarticulate: An Inquiry into the Filipino Understanding of Jesus the Christ.* Manila: Divine Word.

Bergaño, Diego. [1732] 2007. *The Vocabulary of the Kapampangan Language in Spanish and Dictionary of the Spanish Language in Kapampangan: The English Translation of the Kapampangan-Spanish Dictionary.* Angeles City, Philippines: Holy Angel University Press.

Besley, A. C. Tina. 2005. "Self-Denial or Self-Mastery? Foucault's Genealogy of the Confessional Self." *British Journal of Guidance and Counselling* 33 (3): 365–382.

Bialecki, Jon. 2015. "The Judgment of God and the Non-Elephantine Zoo: Christian Dividualism, Individualism, and Ethical Freedom after the Mosko-Robbins Debate." *University of Edinburgh AnthroCyBib Occasional Paper Series.* March 17, 2015. Accessed January 2, 2019. https://www.blogs.hss.ed.ac.uk/anthrocybib/2015/03/17/occasional-paper-bialecki-the-judgment-of-god-and-the-non-elephantine-zoo/.

Bialecki, Jon, Naomi Haynes, and Joel Robbins. 2008. "The Anthropology of Christianity." *Religion Compass* 2 (6): 1139–1158.

Blair, Emma Helen, and James Alexander Robertson, trans. 1903. *The Philippine Islands, 1493–1803.* 55 vols. Cleveland, OH: Arthur H. Clark Co.

Blanco, John D. 2009. *Frontier Constitutions: Christianity and Colonial Empire in the Nineteenth-Century Philippines.* Berkeley: University of California Press.

Bräunlein, Peter J. 2009. "Negotiating Charisma: The Social Dimension of Philippine Crucifixion Rituals." *Asian Journal of Social Science* 37 (6): 892–917.

———. 2010a. *Passion/Pasyon: Rituale des Schmerzes im europäischen und philippinischen Christentum.* Germany: Fink Wilhelm Gmbh + Co.Kg.

———. 2010b. "Flagellation." In *Religions of the World: A Comprehensive Encyclopedia of Beliefs and Practices,* edited by Martin Baumann and J. Gordon Melton, 1121–1122. Santa Barbara, CA: ABC Clio.

Brewer, Carolyn. 2004. "Confession and Flagellation: The Creation of Self-Policing Subjects." In *Shamanism, Catholicism, and Gender Relations in Colonial Philippines, 1521–1685,* 62–79. Aldershot, UK: Ashgate.

Briones, Nikki. 2010. "From War Dance to Theatre of War: Moro-Moro Performances in the Philippines." PhD. diss., National University of Singapore.

Bulloch, Hannah C. M. 2016. "Fetal Personhood in the Christian Philippines: The View from a Visayan Island." *Philippine Studies: Historical and Ethnographic Viewpoints* 64 (2): 195–222.

Bulatao, Jaime, and Vataliano Gorospe. 1966. *Split Level Christianity*. Quezon City, Philippines: Anteneo de Manila University Press.

Bynum, Caroline Walker. 1987. *Holy Feast and Holy Fast the Religious Significance of Food to Medieval Women*. Berkeley: University of California Press.

Cannell, Fenella. 1995. "The Imitation of Christ in Bicol, Philippines." *Journal of the Royal Anthropological Institute* 1 (2): 377–394.

——. 1999. *Power and Intimacy in the Christian Philippines*. New York: Cambridge University Press.

——. ed. 2006. *The Anthropology of Christianity*. Durham, NC: Duke University Press.

Cantillas, Precioso. 2005. "Pastoral Letter: Message of the 19th National Migrant's Sunday." Catholic Bishops Conference of the Philippines. Accessed January 2, 2019. http://www.cbcponline.net/ecmi/letters/19th%20National%20Migrants%20Sunday.htm.

Carr, Lorraine. 1966. *To the Philippines with Love*. Los Angeles, CA: Sherbourne Press.

Carrithers, Michael, Steven Collins, and Steven Lukes, eds. 1985. *The Category of the Person: Anthropology, Philosophy, History*. Cambridge: Cambridge University Press.

Carroll, Michael. 2002. *The Penitent Brotherhood: Patriarchy and Hispano-Catholicism in New Mexico*. Baltimore, MD: Johns Hopkins University Press.

Castro, Alex. 2007a. "Theatre of the Mind." *Views from the Pampang*. March 21. Accessed December 20, 2018. http://viewsfromthepampang.blogspot.sg/2007/03/3-theater-of-mind.html.

——. 2007b. "PASIUN: Sing a Song of Passion." *Views from the Pampang*. August 5. Accessed December 20, 2018. http://viewsfromthepampang.blogspot.com/2007/08/43-pasiun-sing-song-of-passion.html.

——. 2007c. "LIMBUN: The Pageantry of Processions." *Views from the Pampang*. August 21. Accessed September 11, 2017. http://viewsfromthepampang.blogspot.jp/2007/08/45-limbun-pageantry-of-processions.html.

Catholic Bishops Conference of the Philippines (CBCP). 2012. "The Catholic Directory of the Philippines (2010–2011)." Catholic Bishops Conference of the Philippines, 2012. Accessed January 11, 2019. https://newsinfo.inquirer.net/463377/filipino-catholic-population-expanding-say-church-officials.

——.2014. "Pastoral Letter on Filipino Spirituality (Landas ng Pagkabanal)." Catholic Bishops Conference of the Philippines, 19998. Accessed January 2, 2019. http://cbcponline.net/v2/?p=432.

The Catholic Encyclopedia. 1936. New York: Gilmary Society, 1936.

Celano, Thomas of. 2000. *The First Life of St Francis of Assisi*. London: Society for Promoting Christian Knowledge Holy Trinity Church.

Center for Kapampangan Studies (CKS). 2002. "Birthplace of the Vernacular Zarzuela" *Singing* 2 (2): 13.

Chadwick, Harold. 1999. *The Imitation of Christ: Rewritten and Updated*. Plainfield, NJ: Bridge-Logos.

Chakrabarty, Dipesh. 2000. *Provincializing Europe: Postcolonial Thought and Historical Difference*. Princeton, NJ: Princeton University Press.

Chan, Margaret. 2006. *Ritual Is Theatre, Theatre Is Ritual: Tang-ki: Chinese Spirit Medium Worship*. Singapore: Wee Kim Wee Centre, Singapore Management University.

Chirino, Pedro. [1604] 1969. *Relacion de las islas Filipinas*. Manila: Historical Conservation Society.

Choy, Catherine Ceniza. 2003. *Empire of Care: Nursing and Migration in Filipino American History*. Durham, NC: Duke University Press.

Clendinnen, Inga. 1990. "Ways to the Sacred: Reconstructing 'Religion' in Sixteenth-Century Mexico." *History and Anthropology* 5:104–141.

Clooney, Francis X. 2010. *Comparative Theology: Deep Learning across Religious Borders*. Malden, MA: Wiley-Blackwell.

Coakley, Sarah. 2009. "Divine Pain." Interviewed in the radio program *Encounter*. July 26. Australia: ABC Radio National. http://www.abc.net.

Cohn, Norman. 1970. *The Pursuit of the Millennium: Revolutionary Millenarians and Mystical Anarchists of the Middle Ages*. New York: Oxford University Press.

Collins, Elizabeth Fuller. 1997. *Pierced by Murugan's Lance: Ritual, Power, and Moral R edemption among Malaysian Hindus*. Dekalb: Northern Illinois Press.

Collins, Randall. 2004. *Interaction Ritual Chains*. Princeton N.J.: Princeton University Press.

Comaroff, Jean, and John L. Comaroff. 1999a. "Occult Economies and the Violence of Abstraction: Notes from the South African Postcolony." *American Ethnologist* 26 (2): 279–303.

———. 1999b. *On Personhood: An Anthropological Perspective from Africa*. Chicago, IL: American Bar Foundation.

Commission on Filipinos Overseas (CFO). 2012. "Stock Estimate of Overseas Filipinos." Accessed April 14, 2014. http://www.cfo.gov.ph.

Constable, Nicole. 2007. *Maid to Order in Hong Kong: Stories of Migrant Workers*. Ithaca, NY: Cornell University Press.

Cornelio, Jayeel. 2016. *Being Catholic in the Contemporary Philippines: Young People Reinterpreting Religion*. London: Routledge.

Cruz, Aurora. 1991. "Easter? What Easter?" *Malaya Newspaper*, March 31. Accessed from the archives of Ateneo de Manila University Rizal Library.

Cruz, Oscar. 1999. "Pastoral Exhortation on Philippine Culture." CBCP Pastoral Documents. January 25. http://www.cbcponline.net.

Cuming, G. J. 1978. *Studies in Church History*. Edinburgh: Thomas Nelson and Sons.

Cuyno, Jammi, Susane Gutierrez, and Morella Takeno. 2005. "The Role of the Navarro Family in the Continuing Culture of Crucifixion in Cutud, San Fernando Pampanga: An Exploratory Study." Master's thesis, Assumption College, Manila, Philippines.

Damian, Saint Peter. 1959. *Selected Writings on the Spiritual Life*. London: Faber and Faber.

Das, Veena, Arthur Kleinman, and Margaret M. Lock. 1997. *Social Suffering*. Berkeley: University of California Press.

De Belen, Gaspar Aquino. [1704] 1999. *Mahal na passion ni Jesu Christong panginoon natin na tola*. Manila: Ateneo De Manila University Press.

De Guia, Katrin. 2008. "Indigenous Filipino Values: A Foundation for a Culture of Non-Violence." Proceedings of a presentation at the *Forum towards a Culture of Non-Violence*, March 5, Rizal Technological University, Boni Campus in Mandaluyong City, Philippines.

De Guzman, Arnel F. 1993. "Katas ng Saudi: The Work and Life Situation of the Filipino Contract Workers in Saudi Arabia." *Philippine Social Sciences Review* 51 (1–4): 1–56.

de la Cruz, Deirdre. 2015. *Mother Figured: Marian Apparitions and the Making of a Filipino Universal*. Chicago, IL: University of Chicago Press.

De Mesa, José M. 1979. *And God Said, "Bahala Na": The Theme of Providence in the Lowland Filipino Context.* Quezon City: Publisher's Printing Press.

———. 1987. *In Solidarity with the Culture: Studies in Theological Re-Rooting.* Quezon City, Philippines: Maryhill.

———. 2012. "Inculturation as Pilgrimage." In *Mission and Culture: The Louis J. Luzbetak Lectures,* edited by Stephen Bevans, 5–33. American Society of Missiology Series 48. New York: Orbis Books.

Derrida, Jacques. 1976. *Of Grammatology.* Baltimore, MD: Johns Hopkins University Press.

D'Oingt, Marguerite. 1990. *The Writings of Margaret of Oingt, Medieval Prioress and Mystic (d. 1310).* Woodbridge, UK: Boydell & Brewer.

Dorries, H. 1962. "The Place of Confession in Ancient Monasticism." In *Studia patristica,* vol. 5, part III, edited by Cross F. L International Conference on Patristic Studies. Berlin: Akademie-Verlag.

Droysen, Johann Gustav. [1893] 2015. *Outline of the Principles of History (Grundriss der Historik).* London: Forgotten Books.

Dubet, F. 1994. "The System, the Actor, and the Social Subject." *Thesis Eleven* 38:16–35.

Durkheim, Émile. [1912] 2008. *The Elementary Forms of the Religious Life.* Edited by Mark Sydney Cladis. Translated by Carol Cosman. Oxford: Oxford University Press.

Ellwood, Robert S. 1988. *The History and Future of Faith: Religion Past, Present, and to Come.* New York: Crossroad.

Enfield, Nicholas James. 2013. *Relationship Thinking: Agency, Enchrony, and Human Sociality.* Oxford: Oxford University Press.

Ericta, Carmen. 2010. "The 2010 Census of Population and Housing." Republic of the Philippines Statistics Authority, April 4, 2012. https://psa.gov.ph/content /2010-census-population-and-housing-reveals-philippine-population-9234-million.

———. 2013. "Total Number of OFWs Is Estimated at 2.2 Million (Results from the 2012 Survey on Overseas Filipinos)." National Statistics Office of the Philippines. July 11. Accessed December 15, 2013. http://www.census.gov.ph.

Evangelista, Alfredo. 1962. "Penitential Flagellation: The Ritual and the Motives." *Sunday Times Magazine* (Manila), April 15, 10–11. Reprinted in F. Landa Jocano. 1981. *Folk Christianity.* Quezon City, Philippines: Monograph Series No. 1, Manila: Trinity Research Institute.

FABC Theological Advisory Commission. 1991. "Theses on the Local Church." Federation of Asian Bishops Conference (FABC). FABC Paper Number 60. http://www. fabc.org/fabc%20papers/fabc_paper_60.pdf.

Fabella, Virginia. 1999. "Inculturating the Gospel: The Philippine Experience." *The Way* 39 (2): 118–128.

Fabian, Johannes. 1983. *Time and the Other: How Anthropology Makes Its Object.* New York: Columbia University Press.

Fajardo, Kale Bantigue. 2011. *Filipino Crosscurrents: Oceanographies of Seafaring, Masculinities, and Globalization.* Minneapolis: University of Minnesota Press.

Faubion, James D. 2011. *An Anthropology of Ethics.* Cambridge: Cambridge University Press.

Feld, Steven. 1990. "Wept Thoughts: The Voicing of Kaluli Memories." *Oral Tradition* 5 (2–3): 241–266.

———. 1996. "Waterfalls of Song: An Acoustemology of Place Resounding in Bosavi, Papua New Guinea." In *Senses of Place,* edited by Steven Feld and Keith Basso, 91–135. Santa Fe, NM: School of American Research Press.

Fernandez, Doreen. 1996. *Palabas: Essays on Philippine Theater History*. Quezon City, Philippines: Ateneo de Manila University Press.

Fiebach, Joachim. 2002. "Theatricality: From Oral Traditions to Televised "Realities." *SubStance* 31 (2): 17–41.

Fine, Gary Alan. 2005. "Interaction Ritual Chains (Review)." *Social Forces* 83 (3): 1287–1288.

Flannery, Austin. 1984. *Vatican II: Ad Gentes Divinitus*. Harrison, Philippines: Daughters of Saint Paul.

Fogelson, Raymond D. 1982. "Person, Self, and Identity: Some Anthropological Retrospects, Circumspects, and Prospects." In *Psychosocial theories of the self*, edited by Benjamin Lee, 67–109. New York: Plenum.

Foucault, Michel. 1986. "The Cultivation of the Self." In *The History of Sexuality*, vol. 3, *The Care of the Self*. London: Penguin.

——. [1978] 1990. *The History of Sexuality*. Vol. 1, *An Introduction*. Reissue edition. New York: Vintage.

——. 1997a. "Technologies of the Self." In *Ethics: Subjectivity and Truth*, edited by Paul Rabinow, . 253–252. New York: New Press; distributed by W. W. Norton.

——. 1997b. "The Ethics of the Concern for Self as a Practice of Freedom." In *Michel Foucault: Ethics, Subjectivity and Truth, the Essential Works of Michel Foucault, 1954–1984*, edited by Paul Rabinow, 1: 281–302. London: Penguin Press.

——. 2001. *The Hermeneutics of the Subject: Lectures at the Collège de France, 1981–1982*. Edited by Frédéric Gros, François Ewald, and Alessandro Fontana. New York: Palgrave-Macmillan.

Fountain, Philip, and Sin Wen Lau. 2013. "Anthropological Theologies: Engagements and Encounters." *Australian Journal of Anthropology* 24 (3): 227–34.

Franco, Jean. 2011. "The Politics of Language in Labor Export: A Discourse Historical Analysis of Bagong Bayani and Overseas Employment Policies."PhD diss., University of the Philippines.

Fredricks, Rand. 2012. *Fasting: An Exceptional Human Experience*. San Jose, CA: All Things Well Publications.

Gell, Alfred. (1998) 2013. *Art and Agency: An Anthropological Theory*. Oxford: Clarendon Press.

Glucklich, Ariel. 1998. "Sacred Pain and the Phenomenal Self." *Harvard Theological Review* 91 (4): 389–412.

——. 2001. *Sacred Pain: Hurting the Body for the Sake of the Soul*. Oxford: Oxford University Press.

——. 2009. "Divine Pain." Interviewed in the radio program *Encounter*, July 26. Australia: ABC Radio National. http://www.abc.net.au.

Goffman, Erving. [1959] 1990. *The Presentation of Self in Everyday Life*. London: Puffin.

——. [1967] 2003. *Interaction Ritual: Essays on Face-to-Face Behavior*. New York: Pantheon Books.

Gonzalez, Jboy, SJ. 2010. "The Flagellants and Kristos of Lent: Simple Folks Keep the Faith." The Faith of a Centurion: Homilies for Believers Willing to Take Risks. April 1. Accessed November 6, 2012. http://faithofacenturion.blogspot.com.

Gorski, Philip S., and Ateş Altınordu. 2008. "After Secularization?" *Annual Review of Sociology* 34 (1): 55–85.

Gripaldo, Rolando M. 2005. *Filipino Cultural Traits: Claro R. Ceniza Lectures*. Cultural Heritage and Contemporary Change, vol. 4. Washington, DC: Council for Research in Values and Philosophy.

Guevarra, Anna Romina. 2010. *Marketing Dreams, Manufacturing Heroes the Transnational Labor Brokering of Filipino Workers*. New Brunswick, NJ: Rutgers University Press.

Gupta, Akhil, and James Ferguson. 1992. "Beyond 'Culture': Space, Identity, and the Politics of Difference." In *Culture, Power, Place: Explorations in Critical Anthropology*, edited by Akhil Gupta and James Ferguson, 33–51. Durham, NC: Duke University Press.

Halpern, Jodi. 2001. *From Detached Concern to Empathy: Humanizing Medical Practice*. Oxford: Oxford University Press.

Hann, Chris. 2012. "Personhood, Christianity, Modernity." *Anthropology of This Century Online*, vol. 3. Accessed January 2, 2019. http://aotcpress.com.

Hatfield, Elaine, John T. Cacioppo, and Richard L. Rapson. 1994. *Emotional Contagion*. Cambridge: Cambridge University Press.

Hau, Caroline. 2004. *On the Subject of the Nation: Filipino Writings from the Margins, 1981–2004*. Quezon City, Philippines: Ateneo de Manila University Press.

Helmreich, Stefan. 2010. "Listening against Soundscapes." *Anthropology News* 51 (9): 10.

Hermann, Elfriede. 2011. "Empathy, Ethnicity and the Self among the Banbans in Fiji." In *The Anthropology of Empathy*, edited by Douglas Wood Hollan and C. Jason Throop, 25–42. New York: Berghahn Books.

Hess, Sabine. 2006. "Strathern's Melanesian 'Dividual' and the Christian 'Individual': A Perspective from Vanua Lave, Vanuatu." *Oceania* 76:285–296.

Hirschkind, Charles. 2006. *The Ethical Soundscape Cassette Sermons and Islamic Counterpublics*. New York: Columbia University Press.

Hollan, Douglas Wood, and C. Jason Throop, eds. 2011. *The Anthropology of Empathy: Experiencing the Lives of Others in Pacific Societies*. New York: Berghahn Books.

Hughes-Freeland, Felicia, ed. 1998. "From Ritualization to Performativity: The Concheros of Mexico." In *Ritual, Performance, Media*, 85–103. London: Routledge.

Humphrey, Caroline. 1997. "Exemplars and Rules: Aspects of the Discourse of Morality in Mongolia." In *The Ethnography of Moralities*, edited by Signe Howell, 25–48. London: Routledge.

Husserl, Edmund. [1913] 1970. *Logical Investigations*. Translated by J. N. Findlay. New York: Humanities Press.

Ileto, Reynaldo Clemena. 1979. *Pasyon and Revolution: Popular Movements in the Philippines, 1840–1910*. Manila: Ateneo de Manila University Press.

———.1998. *Filipinos and Their Revolution: Event, Discourse, and Historiography*. Quezon City: Ateneo de Manila University Press.

Ingold, Tim. 2011. *Being Alive: Essays on Movement, Knowledge, and Description*. London: Routledge.

International Organization for Migration (IOM). 2013. "Country Migration Report: The Philippines 2013." Accessed April 14, 2014. http://www.iom.int.

Irving, D. R. M. 2010. *Colonial Counterpoint: Music in Early Modern Manila*. Oxford University Press.

Jackson, Michael. 1989. *Paths toward a Clearing: Radical Empiricism and Ethnographic Inquiry*. Bloomington: Indiana University Press.

Jaeger, Werner. 1985. *Early Christianity and Greek Paideia*. Repr. ed. Cambridge, MA: Belknap Press.

Jaeger, Werner, and Gilbert Highet. 1986. *Paideia the Ideals of Greek Culture*. New York: Oxford University Press.

Jenkins, Philip. 2002. *The Next Christendom : The Coming of Global Christianity*. Oxford: Oxford University Press.

Jennings, Nathan G. 2010. *Theology as Ascetic Act: Disciplining Christian Discourse*. 1st ed. New York: Peter Lang International Academic Publishers.

Joaquin, Nick. 1987. "The Native Good Friday: Why It Outranks Easter." *Manila Times*, April 17.

Johnson, Mark, and Pnina Werbner. 2010. Introduction to "Diasporic Encounters, Sacred Journeys: Ritual, Normativity and the Religious Imagination among International Asian Migrant Women." Special issue, *Asia Pacific Journal of Anthropology* 11 (3–4): 205–218.

Kelman, A. V. 2010. "Rethinking the Soundscape: A Critical Genealogy of a Key Term in Sound Studies." *Senses and Society* 5 (2): 212–234.

Kempis, Thomas à. [1494] 2012. *The Imitation Of Christ*. Altenmünster, Germany: Jazzybee Verlag.

Koning, Juliet. 2009. "Singing Yourself into Existence: Chinese Indonesian Entrepreneurs, Pentecostal-Charismatic Christianity and the Indonesian Nation State." In *Christianity and the State in Asia: Complicity and Conflict*, edited by Julius Bautista and Francis Lim Khek Gee, 115–130. New York: Routledge.

Kreuder, Friedman. 2008. "Flagellation of the Son of God and Divine Flagellation: Flagellator Ceremonies and Flagellation Scenes in the Medieval Passion Play." *Theatre Research International* 33 (2): 176–190.

Laidlaw, James. 1995. *Riches and Renunciation: Religion, Economy, and Society among the Jains*. Oxford: Clarendon Press.

Laksana, Albertus. 2014. *Muslim and Catholic Pilgrimage Practices: Explorations through Java*. Farnham, UK: Ashgate.

Largier, Niklaus. 2007. *In Praise of the Whip*. New York: Zone Books; distributed by MIT Press.

Larkin, John A. 1972. *The Pampangans; Colonial Society in a Philippine Province*. Berkeley: University of California Press.

Latour, Bruno. 2005. *Reassembling the Social an Introduction to Actor-Network-Theory*. Oxford: Oxford University Press.

Law, John, and John Hassard. 1999. *Actor-Network Theory and After*. Oxford: Blackwell / Sociological Review.

Lee, T. S. 1999. "Technology and the Production of Islamic Space: The Call to Prayer in Singapore." *Ethnomusicology* 43 (1): 86–100.

Legaspi, Leonardo Z. 1988. "Pastoral Letter of the Catholic Bishops' Conference of the Philippines on the Occasion of National Migration Day." Catholic Bishops Conference of the Philippines. February 21. Accessed December 14, 2013. http://www.cbcponline.net.

Lindquist, Johan, Biao Xiang, and Brenda S. A. Yeoh. 2012. "Opening the Black Box of Migration: Brokers, the Organization of Transnational Mobility and the Changing Political Economy in Asia." *Pacific Affairs* 85 (1): 7–19.

Lipps, Theodore, 1903. "Einfühlung, Innere Nachahmung und Organempfindung." *Archiv für gesamte Psychologie* 1:465–519. Translated as "Empathy, Inner Imitation and Sense-Feelings," in *A Modern Book of Esthetics*, 374–382. New York: Holt, Rinehart and Winston.

Lopez, Gregorio. 1605. "The Annual Letter of the Vice-Province of the Philippines, June 1604 to June 1605" (RASJ) Phil. 5, ff. 171–195; trans. Repetti, 1949. "The Society of Jesus in the Philippines, 1604–1605." Unpublished manuscript. Washington, DC: Georgetown University.

Lopez, Mario. 2012. "Progressive Entanglements: Religious Intimacy in Japanese-Filipino Marriages." *Philippine Studies: Ethnographic and Historical Viewpoints* 60 (2): 261–290.

Love, Robert S. 2004. *The Samahan of Papa God : Tradition and Conversion in a Tagalog Peasant Religious Movement.* Manila: Anvil Publishing.

Loyola, St. Ignatius. 2007. *The Spiritual Exercises of St Ignatius of Loyola.* New York: Cosimo.

Lumbera, Bienvenido. 1986. *Tagalog Poetry, 1570–1898: Tradition and Influences in Its Development.* Quezon City, Philippines: Ateneo de Manila University Press.

Macarain, Evelyn. 2009. "Nazarene March: 227 Hurt." *Philippine Star,* January 10.

Magsanoc, Letty J. 1977. "Lent's Delirium." *Bulletin Today,* April 8.

Makeniman. 2007. "Views from the Pampang: Theatres of the Mind." *Views from the Pampang.* March 21. Accessed June 12, 2012. http://viewsfromthepampang.blogspot.sg.

Mauss, Marcel. (1935) 1973. "Techniques of the Body." *Economy and Society* 2 (1): 70–88.

Mayblin, Maya. 2014. "The Untold Sacrifice: The Monotony and Incompleteness of Self-Sacrifice in Northeast Brazil." *Ethnos: Journal of Anthropology* 79 (3): 342–364.

Mayblin, Maya, and Magnus Course. 2014. Introduction to "The Other Side of Sacrifice." Special issue, *Ethnos: Journal of Anthropology* 79 (3): 307–319.

McAndrew, John P. 2001. *People of Power: A Philippine Worldview of Spirit Encounters.* Quezon City, Philippines: Ateneo de Manila University Press.

McDougall, Debra. 2009. "Rethinking Christianity and Anthropology: A Review Article." *Anthropological Forum* 19 (2): 185–194.

McKay, Dierdre. 2013. *The Virtual Village: Coping with a Global World.* Bloomington: Indiana University Press.

McKay, Steven. 2011. "Re-Masculinizing the Hero: Filipino Migrant Men and Gender Privilege." Working Paper Series Number 172, Asia Research Institute, National University of Singapore.

Medina, Juan de. (1630) 1893. *Historia de los sucesos de la Orden de N. Gran P. S. Agustin de estas Islas Filipinas.* Manila: Chofrey y Comp.

Mellor, Philip A. 1991. "Self and Suffering: Deconstruction and Reflexive Definition in Buddhism and Christianity." *Religious Studies* 27 (1): 49–63.

Mercado, Leonardo N. 1974. *Elements of Filipino Philosophy.* Tacloban, Philippines: Divine Word University Publications.

———. 1994. "Loob, Body, Self, Bait." In *The Filipino Mind,* 2:19–40. Washington, DC: Council for Research in Values and Philosophy.

Merleau-Ponty, Maurice. 1964. *Sense and Nonsense.* Translated by Herbet L. Dreyfus and Patricia Allen Dreyfus. Evanston, IL: Northwestern University Press.

Miranda, Dionisio. 1989. *Loob—The Filipino Within: A Preliminary Investigation into a Pre-Theological Moral Anthropology.* Manila: Divine Word Publications.

Mirano, Elena Rivera. 1992. *Musika: An Essay on the Spanish Influence on Philippine Music.* Manila: Sentrong Pangkultura ng Pilipinas.

Morelos, Carmelo, D.D. 1995. " 'Comfort My People, Comfort Them' (Isaias 40:1): A Pastoral Letter on Filipino Migrant Workers." Catholic Bishops' Conference of the Philippines, Media Office. July 10. Accessed December 14, 2013. http://cbcponline.net.

Mosko, Mark. 2010. "Partible Penitents: Dividual Personhood and Christian Practice in Melanesia and the West." *Journal of the Royal Anthropological Institute* 16 (2): 215–240.

Muehlebach, Andrea. 2012. *The Moral Neoliberal: Welfare and Citizenship in Italy.* Chicago, IL: University of Chicago Press.

———. 2013. "The Catholicization of Neoliberalism: On Love and Welfare in Lombardy, Italy." *American Anthropologist* 115 (3): 452–465.

Murray, Alison. 1988. "The European Medieval and Philippine Pagan Elements of Holy Week in the Philippines." Unpublished thesis, University of the Philippines, Diliman.

Napolitano, Valentina, and Kristin Norget. 2009."Economies of Sanctity." *Postscripts* 5 (3): 251–264.

National Statistics Office of the Philippines (NSO). 2015. "The 2015 Census of Population and Housing." Philippine Statistics Authority. Accessed September 19, 2017. https://psa.gov.ph.

Navarro, Nelson. 1991. "Lenten Madness." *Malaya*, March 28.

Oder, Slawomir, and Saverio Gaeta. 2010. *Why He Is a Saint: The Life and Faith of Pope John Paul II and the Case for Canonization.* New York: Rizzoli.

Ong, Aihwa. 2006. *Neoliberalism as Exception: Mutations in Citizenship and Sovereignty.* Durham, NC: Duke University Press.

Orejas, Tonette. 2005. "Getting Nailed For Good Friday." Philippine Daily Inquirer News Service. March 25. Accessed June 12, 2013. http://baptistwatch.websitetoolbox.com.

———. 2010. "A Serious Look at Pampanga Crucifixion Rites." *Planet Philippines,* March 30. http://planetphilippines.com.

———. 2012. "Prelate Refutes Book's Assertions on Pampanga Clergy." *Philippine Daily Inquirer,* June 24. http://newsinfo.inquirer.net.

———. 2013. "Young Flagellants Abound in Cutud on Good Friday." *Philippine Daily Inquirer,* March 17. http://newsinfo.inquirer.nety.

Palma-Beltran, Ruby. 1991. "Filipino Women Domestic Helpers Overseas: Profile and Implications for Policy." *Asian Migrant* 4 (2): 46–52.

Panganiban, Patricia G. "Inculturation and the Second Vatican Council." *Landas: Journal of Loyola School of Theology* 18 (1): 59–93.

Pangilinan, Maria Lourdes Carmella Jade. 2015. *Kasalesayan Ning San Fernando.* San Fernando, CA: City Government of San Fernando.

Parreñas, Rhacel Salazar. 2008. *The Force of Domesticity: Filipina Migrants and Globalization.* New York: New York University Press.

Parsons, Talcott. 1951. *The Social System.* Glencoe, IL: Free Press.

Pavia, Joey. 2012. "Pampanga Cited for Efforts to Help OFW Residents." *Business Mirror,* November 28.

Peirano, Mariza G. S. 1998. "When Anthropology Is at Home: The Different Contexts of a Single Discipline." *Annual Review of Anthropology* 27 (1): 105–128.

Penson, Maximo. 1917. "Superstitious Beliefs from Our Town (San Miguel Bulacan)." *Tagalog Ethnography Series* 3:147. Manila: Beyer Collection.

Perkins, Judith. 1995. *The Suffering Self: Pain and Narrative Representation in Early Christian Era.* London: Routledge.

Pertierra, Raul. 1988. *Religion, Politics, and Rationality in a Philippine Community.* Quezon City, Philippines: Ateneo de Manila University Press.

———. ed. 1992. *Remittances and Returnees: The Cultural Economy of Migration in Ilocos.* Quezon City, Philippines: New Day Publishers.

Peterson, William. 2016. *Places for Happiness: Community, Self, and Performance in the Philippines.* Honolulu: University of Hawai'i Press.

Pew Forum. 2011. "Global Christianity—A Report on the Size and Distribution of the World's Christian Population." Pew Forum on Religion and Public Life. December 19. Accessed September 19, 2017. http://www.pewforum.org.

Phelan, John Leddy. [1959] 2011. *The Hispanization of the Philippines Spanish Aims and Filipino Responses, 1565–1700*. Madison: University of Wisconsin Press.

Philippine Statistics Authority (PSA). 2012. "The Pinoy Diaspora: Where Do Our OFWs Come From and Where Do They Go?" Philippine Statistics Authority. May 16. Accessed April 14, 2014. http://www.nscb.gov.ph.

Pinault, David. 1993. *The Shiites: Ritual and Popular Piety in a Muslim Community*. New York: St. Martin's.

Pinggol, Alicia. 2001. *Remaking Masculinities: Identity, Power, and Gender Dynamics in Families with Migrant Wives and Househusbands*. Quezon City, Philippines: University of the Philippines Center for Women's Studies.

Pope John XXIII. 1962. "Encyclical Paenitentiam Agere of John XXIII, 1st July 1962." Vatican.com. July 1. http://www.vatican.va.

Porath, Nathan. 2008. "Seeing Sound: Consciousness and Therapeutic Acoustics in the Inter-sensory Shamanic Epistemology of the Orang Sakai of Riau (Sumatra)." *Journal of the Royal Anthropological Institute* 14:647–663.

Punay, Edu. 2008. "Flagellation, Crucifixion against Church Teachings- Bishop." *Philippine Star*, March 18.

Quevedo, Orlando. 2000. "Missions and the Church in the Philippines: A Pastoral Letter on the Church's Mission in the New Millennium." Catholic Bishop's Conference of the Philippines website, July 5. http://cbcponline.net/v2/?p=453.

Radcliffe-Brown, A. R. 1964. *The Andaman Islanders*. New York: Free Press.

Rafael, Vicente L. 1988. *Contracting Colonialism: Translation and Christian Conversion in Tagalog Society under Early Spanish Rule*. Ithaca, NY: Cornell University Press.

———. 2000. *White Love and Other Events in Filipino History*. Durham, NC: Duke University Press.

Republic of the Philippines Presidential Management Staff (PMS). 1992. *The Aquino Management of the Presidency: Her People's Emissary*. Manila: Office of the President of the Philippines.

Ribadeneira, Marcelo de. (1601) 1947. *Historia de las Islas del Archipelago Filipino y reinos de la Gran China, Tartaria, Cochinchina, Malaca, Siam, Combodge Y Japon*. Edited by Juan R. de Legisima. Madrid: Historical Conservation Society.

Robbins, Joel, and Alan Rumsey. 2008. "Introduction: Cultural and Linguistic Anthropology and the Opacity of Other Minds." *Anthropological Quarterly* 81 (2): 407–420.

Rodriguez, Robyn. 2006. "Migrant Heroes: Nationalism, Citizenship and the Politics of Filipino Migrant Labor." *Citizenship Studies* 6 (3): 341–356.

———. 2010. *Migrants for Export How the Philippine State Brokers Labor to the World*. Minneapolis: University of Minnesota Press.

Rooke, M. 2008. *Decoding Christianity: Flesh and Blood*. Dublin: Tile Films. http://www.youtube.com.

Rosales, Gaudencio. 2004. "Lent and Holy Week and the Passion of the Christ." Pastoral Letter of the Roman Catholic Archdiocese of Manila. March 25. Accessed September 7, 2009. http://www.rcam.org/news/passionofthechrist-2.htm.

Rostas, Susanna. 1998. "From Ritualization to Performativity: The Concheros of Mexico." In *Ritual, Performance, Media*, edited by Felicia Hughes-Freeland, 85–103. London: Routledge.

Rubin, Miri. 1991. *Corpus Christi: The Eucharist in Late Medieval Culture*. Cambridge: Cambridge University Press.

Rudnyckyj, Daromir. 2009. "Spiritual Economies: Islam and Neoliberalism in Contemporary Indonesia." *Cultural Anthropology* 24 (1): 104–141.

Samuels, D. W., L. Meintjes, A. Ochoa, and T. Porcello. 2010. "Soundscapes: Toward a Sounded Anthropology." *Annual Review of Anthropology* 39:329–345.

Sanburn, Josh. 2010. "Top 10 Ridiculously Violent Movies." *Time*, September 2. http://entertainment.time.

Sanneh, Lamin, and Joel A. Carpenter. 2005. *The Changing Face of Christianity: Africa, the West, and the World*. Oxford: Oxford University Press.

Santa Maria, Felice. 1989. "Passion Power (26 March 1986)." In *Halupi: Essays on Philippine Culture*, edited by Corazon Alvina and Felice Santa Maria. Quezon City, Philippines: Capitol Publishing House.

Santiago, Luciano. 2002. *Laying the Foundations: Kapampangan Pioneers in the Philippine Church, 1592–2001*. Angeles City, Philippines: Holy Angel University Press.

Sapitula, Manuel. 2013. "Marian Piety and Modernity: A Sociological Assessment of Popular Religion in the Philippines." PhD diss., National University of Singapore.

Sapnu, Ric. 2013. "For 27th Time, Laborer Leads Cutud Crucifixion." *Philippine Star*, March 31. http://www.philstar.com.

Sax, William Sturman, Johannes Quack, and Jan Weinhold. 2010. *The Problem of Ritual Efficacy*. Oxford: Oxford University Press.

Scalice, Joseph Paul. 2009. "Pasyon, Awit, Legend: Reynaldo Ileto"'s Pasyon and Revolution Thirty Years Later: A Critique." Master's thesis, University of California, Berkeley.

Scarry, Elaine. 1985. *The Body in Pain: The Making and Unmaking of the World*. New York: Oxford University Press.

Schafer, R. Murray. 1977. *The Tuning of the World*. New York: Knopf.

———. 1993. *The Soundscape: Our Sonic Environment and the Tuning of the World*. Rochester, VT: Destiny Books.

Scheper-Hughes, Nancy. 1995. "The Primacy of the Ethical: Propositions for a Militant Anthropology." *Current Anthropology* 36 (3): 409–440.

Schumacher, John N. 1979. *Readings in Philippine Church History*. Quezon City, Philippines: Loyola School of Theology, Ateneo de Manila University Press.

Seligman, Adam B., Robert P. Weller, Michael J. Puett, and Bennett Simon. 2008. *Ritual and Its Consequences: An Essay on the Limits of Sincerity*. Oxford: Oxford University Press.

Shaw, Angel Velasco. 1992. *Nailed*. New York: Third World Newsreel. DVD.

Shilling, Chris, and Philip Mellor. 2010. "Saved from Pain or Saved through Pain? Modernity, Instrumentalization and the Religious Use of Pain as a Body Technique." *European Journal of Social Theory* 13:521–537.

Silos, Leonardo. 1985. "Reflections on Tiwala: An Essay in the Philosophy and Theology behind a Tagalog Word." *Kinaadman* 7 (1): 25–37.

Smart, John E., Virginia A. Teodosio, and Carol J. Jimenez. 1986. "Skills and Earnings: Issues in the Developmental Impact on the Philippines of Labor Export to the Middle East." In *Asian Labor Migration: Pipeline to the Middle East*, edited by Fred Arnold and Nasra M. Shah, 101–124. Boulder, CO: Westview Press.

Smith, Jeffrey S. 2000. "Los Hermanos Penitentes: An Illustrative Essay." *North American Geographer* 2 (1): 70–84.

Smith, Tom. 2012. "Beliefs about God across Time and Countries." National Opinion Research Center at the University of Chicago. December 21, 2018. http://www.norc.org/pdfs/beliefs_about_god_report.pdf.

Sokefeld, M. 1999. "Debating Self, Identity, and Culture in Anthropology." *Current Anthropology* 4:417–447.

Solomon, M. Scott. 2009. "State-Led Migration, Democratic Legitimacy, and Deterritorialization: The Philippines' Labour Export Model." *European Journal of East Asian Studies* 8 (2): 275–300.

Stein, Edith. [1917] 1964. *On the Problem of Empathy.* The Hague: Martinus Nijhoff.

Stoller, Paul. 1989. *The Taste of Ethnographic Things: The Senses in Anthropology.* Philadelphia: University of Pennsylvania Press.

Strathern, Marilyn. 1988. The Gender of the Gift: Problems with Women and Problems with Society in Melanesia. Berkeley: University of California Press.

Stueber, Karsten. 2010. *Rediscovering Empathy: Agency, Folk Psychology, and the Human Sciences.* Cambridge, MA: MIT Press.

Tadiar, Neferti X. M. 2009. *Things Fall Away: Philippine Historical Experience and the Makings of Globalization.* Durham, NC: Duke University Press.

Tantingco, Robert. 2006. "Chastity, Compassion, Honor: Kapampangan Traits Now Lost and Forgotten." *SingSing* 4 (2): 6–6.

———. 2010a. "Pampang as Metaphor for Pampanga." *Sun Star,* April 5. http://www.sunstar.com.ph.

———. 2010b. "The Majigangas of Sta. Ana." *Sun Star,* December 21. http://www.sunstar.com.ph.

———. 2012. "Miracle at the Apu Shrine." *Sun Star Pampanga,* April 9. http://www.sunstar.com.ph.

Tantingco, Robert, et al. 2011. *Pinatubo: The Volcano in Our Backyard.* Angeles City, Philippines: Holy Angel University Press.

Taylor, Carl N. 1936. *Odyssey of the Islands.* New York: Charles Scribner's Sons.

Taylor, Charles. 2007. *A Secular Age.* Cambridge, MA: Belknap Press of Harvard University Press.

———. 2008. "Buffered and Porous Selves." The Immanent Frame: Secularism, Religion and the Public Sphere. September 2, 2008. Accessed December 26, 2018. http://blogs.ssrc.org/tif/2008/09/02/buffered-and-porous-selves/.

Tiatco, S. Anril Pineda. 2010. "Libad Nang Apung Iru and Pamamaku King Krus: Performances of Ambivalence in Kapampangan Cultural Spectacles." *Drama Review* 54 (2): 91–102.

———. 2012. "Imag(in)ing Saint Lucy: The Narrative and Performative Construction of the Kuraldal in Sasmuan, Philippines." *Philippine Humanities Review* 14 (1): 124–150.

———. 2016. *Performing Catholicism: Faith and Theater in a Philippine Province.* Quezon City: University of the Philippine Press.

Tiatco, S. Anril Pineda, and Amihan Bonifacio-Ramolete. 2008. "Cutud's Ritual of Nailing on the Cross: Performance of Pain and Suffering." *Asian Theatre Journal* 25:58–76.

Tigno, Jorge. 2012. "Agency by Proxy: Women and the Human Trafficking Discourse in the Philippines." In *Labor Migration and Human Trafficking in Southeast Asia,* edited by Michelle Ford, Lyons Lenore, and Willem van Schendel, 23–40. Oxford: Routledge.

Tiongson, Nicanor G. 1976. "The Pasyon: The Best-Known Filipino Book." *Archipelago* 3:30–38.

Toke, Leslie. 1909. "Flagellants." In *The Catholic Encyclopedia*. New York: Robert Appleton Company. http://www.newadvent.org.

Trembinksi, Donna. 2008. "[Pro]passio Doloris: Early Dominican Conceptions of Christ's Physical Pain." *Journal of Ecclesiastical History* 59 (4): 630–656.

Tremlett, Paul-François. 2006. "Power, Invulnerability, Beauty: Producing and Transforming Male Bodies in the Lowland Chritianised Philippines." School of Oriental and African Studies, University Centre (School of Oriental and African Studies' Centre for Gender and Religion Research). Accessed: July 2, 2018. http://oro.open.ac.uk.

———. 2014. "Urban Religious Change at the Neoliberal Frontier: Notes toward a Spatial Analysis of a Contemporary Filipino Vernacular Catholicism." *Philippine Studies: Historical and Ethnographic Viewpoints* 62 (3): 529–547.

Trimillos, Ric. 1992. "Pasyon: Lenten Observance of the Philippines as Southeast Asian Theater." In *Essays on Southeast Asian Performing Arts: Local Manifestations and Cross-Cultural Implications*, edited by Kathy Foley, 5–22. Berkeley: Center for South and Southeast Asia Studies, University of California at Berkeley.

Trouillot, Michel-Rolph. 1995. *Silencing the Past: Power and the Production of History.* Boston, MA: Beacon Press.

Tubeza, P. C. 2013. "No Crucifixions Please—Prelate." *Philippine Daily Inquirer,* March27. Accessed March 7, 2017. http://newsinfo.inquirer.net.

Tyner, James. 2000. "Migrant Labor and the Politics of Scale: Gendering the Philippine State." *Asia Pacific Viewpoint* 41 (2): 131–154.

Urban, Greg. 1988. "Ritual Wailing in Amerindian Brazil" *American Anthropologist* 90 (2): 385–400.

Uy, Jocelyn. 2013. "Filipino Catholic Population Expanding, Say Church Officials." *Philippine Daily Inquirer,* August 11, "Nation." Accessed January 2, 2019. https://newsinfo.inquirer.net/463377/filipino-catholic-population-expanding-say-church-officials.

Vaez, Francisco, S. J. 1903 [1601]. "'Annual Letters from the Philippine Islands to Reverend Father Claudio Aquaviva, General of the Society of Jesus, 10 June." In *History of the Philippine Islands,* edited by Emma Helen Blair and James Alexander Robertson, 11:196–197. Cleveland, OH: Arthur H. Clark.

Van Der Veer, Peter. 1995. "The Modernity of Religion: The Genealogies of Religion: A Review." *Social History* 20 (3): 365–371.

Villamor, Ignacio, and Felipe Buencamino. 1920. *Census of the Philippine Islands Taken under the Direction of the Philippine Legislature in the Year 1918.* Manila: Bureau of Printing.

Wagner, Roy. 1991. "The Fractal Person." In *Big Men and Great Men: The Personifications of Power,* edited by Maurice Godelier and Marilyn Strathern, 159–173. Cambridge: Cambridge University Press.

Walsh, Michael. 2010. "Pope John Paul Practiced Self-Mortification." *National Catholic Reporter,* February 5. Academic OneFile.

Weber, Max. (1905) 2002. *The Protestant Ethic and the Spirit of Capitalism.* Los Angeles, CA: Roxbury.

Wiegele, Katharine L. 2005. *Investing in Miracles: El Shaddai and the Transformation of Popular Catholicism in the Philippines.* Honolulu: University of Hawai'i Press.

Williamson, John, ed. 1990. *Latin American Adjustment: How Much Has Happened?* Washington, DC: Institute for International Economics.

Wiseman, Theresa. 1996. "A Concept Analysis of Empathy." *Journal of Advanced Nursing* 23:1162–1167.

Wroth, William. 1991. *Images of Penance, Images of Mercy: Southwestern Santos in the Late Nineteenth Century.* Norman: University of Oklahoma Press.

Yepes, Victoria. 1996. *Una etnografía de los indios Bisayas del Padre Alcina.* Madrid: Consejo Superior de Investigaciones Científicas.

Zialcita, Fernando. 1986. "Popular Interpretations of the Passion of Christ." *Philippine Sociological Review* 34 (1–4): 56–62.

———. 2000. *Cuaresma.* Makati, Philippines: Bookmark and Bungang Araw.

JULIUS BAUTISTA is an associate professor at the Center for Southeast Asian Studies, Kyoto University, Japan. He received his PhD in Southeast Asian studies (anthropology and cultural history) at Australian National University, and his research has focused on religious practice in Asia, particularly Christian iconography, religious piety, performance, and the relationship between religion and the state. He is author of *Figuring Catholicism: An Ethnohistory of the Santo Niño de Cebu* (2010), editor of *The Spirit of Things: Materiality and Religious Diversity in Southeast Asia* (2012), and coeditor (with Francis Lim) of *Christianity and the State in Asia: Complicity and Conflict* (2009). He has also published in *The Australian Journal of Anthropology, Cultural Anthropology, Asian Studies Review, Sojourn: Journal of Social Issues in Southeast Asia, The International Journal of Asian Christianity,* and the *Asian Journal of Social Science.*

Made in the USA
Las Vegas, NV
30 January 2024

85110128R00090